MEDITATIONS OF A HERMIT

MEDITATIONS OF A HERMIT

by Charles de Foucauld

Translation by Charlotte Balfour
Preface by René Bazin
Introduction by Algar Thorold

BURNS & OATES – LONDON
ORBIS BOOKS – NEW YORK

First published 1930
Reissued (abridged) 1981
by Burns & Oates Ltd.,
2–10 Jerdan Place, London SW6 5PT

in association with
Orbis Books,
Maryknoll, New York 10545

Copyright 1930 Burns & Oates
Copyright © 1981 Burns & Oates

ISBN (UK) : 0 86012 120 8
ISBN (USA): 0 88344 325 2

Printed in the U.S.A.

PREFACE

By M. RÉNE BAZIN

So many authentic documents were put at my disposal before I began to write the Biography of Charles de Foucauld[1] that I can claim to have followed him almost day by day through his eventful life. I saw him as a Moroccan explorer, as a novice at Notre Dame des Neiges, as a Trappist at Akbès, as the servant of the Poor Clares at Nazareth, at Jerusalem, as a hermit at Béni-Abbès and in the Hoggar, and was even present, through their medium, at his death.

Charles de Foucauld now has friends throughout the world and many amongst them are anxious to know something of the private writings he left to the White Fathers.

All sorts of people have written to me. ' Why,' says one, ' do you not edit the four notebooks of the *Retreat at Nazareth* in 1897 ? ' ' Is the *Essay on the Companionship of Jesus* published yet ? ' Another begs for the *Meditations on the Gospel.* Many would like to see *The Gospel Preached to the Poor of the Sahara,* a collection of thoughts whose title evokes all the Sunshine of the South, its poetry and the sweetness of Christ.

But none of these writings, mentioned either in the last pages of the Biography or in the index of his works, is suitable for publication by itself.

[1] *Charles de Foucauld : Hermit and Explorer.* By René Bazin. Translated by Peter Keelan. London, Burns Oates & Washbourne Ltd.

PREFACE

Not one of them was written for the world's reading. Not one is consecutive. In his rush-thatched hut through the quiet night of the African desert or the Holy Land, Brother Charles would draw the packing-case that was his table up to his little window to save lamp oil, and would write by the light of the stars. He would recapitulate again and again some old theme of meditation, the grandeur and the ways and ramifications of which he had known in the far-off days of La Trappe. Following his own inclinations the meditation would become a colloquy. His mind was nourished by much reading of the Saints, particularly the writings of S. Teresa and S. John of the Cross, and he would apply to his own particular case the doctrines and counsels that he found in them. He was no theologian. But by his experience and love of the Cross, by virtue of his unceasing search after the will of God and his complete self-effacement he was undoubtedly the equal of many masters of this exacting science. Moreover, he was the first to expound, both in theory and in practice, the difficult art of instructing the Mussulmans. He conquered their worldly prejudices by charity and earned blessing from those who were offended by the very name of Christian. He led them gently and tenderly to the truth of which he, Brother Charles, was the one and only voice and witness to those nomad tribes.

One or two of his writings were probably destined by him to those successors to whom, all his life, he appealed in vain. Though none ever joined him in his life on the caravan road, he never failed to note in his diary the depth and the quality of the water and to add, if the supply was pure and steady, ' A Fraternity could well be established here.' One

PREFACE

can imagine the sort of book *The Gospel preached to the Poor of the Sahara* might have been if the wandering hermit, ' the sower whose steps no one had counted,' had been at all the ' author.' We might have had a series of Gospel stories told in the Oriental manner in which the teller would give the atmosphere of his own personality, of the country and of the listeners to his stories, ignorant nomadic people, vivid and cunning. But Brother Charles never thought of writing in this way. The Circulating Library and literary fame were not what he wrote for. All he aimed at was to measure out the small amount of truth that the ' Poor of the Sahara ' were capable of absorbing, just so much light as their blind souls could take in without being startled ; for eyes, unaccustomed to light, will close their lids if too much brightness is shewn to them all at once. He puts the tenets of Christian teaching into that order in which they could be apprehended by the Mussulmans. The twenty-one *Conférences* were written in 1903 at Béni-Abbès. He gave them the sub-title of *A Little Introduction to the Catechism*, and that is just what they are. The whole interest of the work lies in the order in which he puts the subjects he writes of. First he speaks of God. To speak of God as the All Powerful is no offence to the faith of the Mussulman nourished on the Koran ; and here the child of Islam learns that in this he and the Catholic have a common Faith in the One God. Later on, in the Eighth Lesson, the doctrine of the Trinity is unfolded. This is alien to the Mussulman spirit. In the Ninth Lesson the Incarnation is spoken of, and later on come the Laws of God, the Laws of the Church, the meaning of the Cross, and finally the mystery of the Eucharist is revealed to the people of the desert, their minds having been gently led

PREFACE

upwards to this Truth. As I say, in this, only, lies the point of *The Gospel preached to the Poor of the Sahara*. It is as simple in form as a child's catechism, but wherever the name of God is mentioned the author uses the formula of the East, and knowing that the impulse of his heart will be understood by his hearers, he adds : ' Let us praise him. There is no other God but he.' In the Ninth Lesson, where he speaks of the coming into the world of the Son of God made man, he cries again : ' Glory to God. There is no other God but him,' thus summing up and affirming the great doctrines he has just taught of the Trinity, the Incarnation and the Redemption.

Each of the twenty-one lessons begins with the prayer : ' My God, let all men come to Heaven ! ' Charles de Foucauld's charitable heart was afraid that his lessons would not be understood by the desert folk and prayed thus to encourage them.

So, though there is much that is beautiful in these pages, they are clearly not suitable for modern French readers.

It is the same with the five manuscript books entitled : *Essay on the Companionship of Jesus*.

After his conversion Charles de Foucauld never ceased meditating on the Gospels. He had a marvellous knowledge of them. In his little hut at Nazareth he copied out for his own use the texts suitable to every day in the year, beginning by the first Sunday of Advent. Sometimes he joined them together by a few words. He had the country of Galilee before his eyes. He knew it through and through and his knowledge of the geography of the Holy Land shews itself often in his notes of Our Lord's movements.

These words, for instance, occur at the date of

PREFACE

December 21: 'The Blessed Virgin and S. Joseph left Nazareth this morning to go to Bethlehem. They crossed the plain of Esdraelon and probably found food and shelter this night somewhere near Engannim towards Jenin or Zebabda. Always as they go they contemplate Jesus and adore him, day and night, both travelling and resting.'

The Gospel preached to the Poor of the Sahara is therefore not included in this volume of Spiritual Writings which is composed chiefly of extracts from *Meditations on the Gospels* and his correspondence and retreat notes. His retreats encouraged Brother Charles more than anything to perseverance and advance in the spiritual life. He made four retreats before he decided to leave the world and obey the voice which called him to the narrow service of Christ. Every year he made one—at Nazareth, at Jerusalem, at Ephraim, at Béni-Abbès, at In Salah, at Tamanrasset. With his passion for solitude he loved these times—his notebooks are full of the hermit's 'joy at being alone at last'—necessary times for self-examination and renewed resolve. He could look for no help or counsel from man. All around him was moral disintegration, ignorance, pride. For himself and for his flock there were constant grave decisions to be made. Always must he keep peace within, that peace which was his strength, his supreme treasure, bought at the price of having left all things.

At such times he would go apart, shut the door of his hermitage to all visitors and for eight or ten days keep his fervent and attentive soul in the presence of God. He enjoyed the absence of his fellow-creatures and the presence of God.

A poetical note is sometimes struck in the Meditations. He hears the rain falling in Judea, he sees

*

PREFACE

the stars travel over the ways traversed by the shepherds, the Magi, S. John the Baptist and the crowds that acclaimed the Son of Man. But the poetic touches are not frequent in the Spiritual Writings. Perhaps if he had had any idea of writing for a public they would have been more abundant.

That he had a leaning to them is proved by his manner of presenting the sober but varied local colours in his *Reconnaissance au Maroc*, the book he wrote in his youth. There light and shade are balanced with a sure touch. But here we must not look for landscape painting and elaborate passages tuneful to the ear, or for pictures harmoniously linked by choice periods into a net in which the soul is caught up. There is none of the emotion of the ' grand style ' in these pages. They are simply the habitual and familiar prayer of a contemplative. The hermit was writing for himself. He was not afraid to repeat himself, to quote texts and return to his favourite themes and to use over and over again the thoughts and analyses that had become habitual to him. My task has been to select suitable passages, to punctuate and fill in unfinished sentences and words and to give the whole work the coherence that he did not trouble to give it himself.

I should like to point out one particular merit above all others of these spiritual writings. It is that nowhere, in these intimate notes and letters, is there to be found either a word of doubt, or the smallest tendency to enlarge upon the disorders of his past life, or the dangers of the world he had left behind, nor even a word of remorse in which one might detect a certain self-complacency.

I have been through an immense number of jottings and notes of Charles de Foucauld written

PREFACE

between his Conversion and his death and have found in them only the purest sentiments. There were left no smouldering embers of ancient fires. This is very remarkable, and it would seem that this officer of the African Chasseurs was the object of very unusual graces from the moment that he entered unpremeditatedly the confessional of the Abbé Huvelin in the Church of S. Augustin.

I am not in a position to judge of such things, but I feel sure that a great many of my readers have the same impression.

The other characteristics of these writings are a complete, unconquerable faith, a tender piety like that of a child that runs with lifted hands and arms to the one he loves, a humility that is all the more complete that it is founded on a great knowledge of the world, and finally words of courage are found in them that are peculiar to him and which in his case strike a very grand note.

The diversity of the Saints is one of the visible signs of the spiritual riches of the Church. Though they but practise the virtues recommended to all Christians, they each put into their practice something of their own temperament, of their breeding, of their special calling or vocation and particularly of the special and peculiar graces given to each. As no two leaves are alike on the same tree, so no two Saints are alike. Charles de Foucauld had two manners of expression which are worthy to be stored in those open granaries where all may come to gather true wholesome grain thrashed out ready for the sowing.

He has lovely words of salutation for the Angels, or the Saints, or the Blessed Virgin, above all for the Master whose humble friend and knight he was. He was a knight by baptism as are all men, but his

PREFACE

ancestry spoke in him and urged him on. Relatives and comrades have told me that he never knew fear, either as a child or as soldier, Trappist or hermit. Many uplifting sayings are scattered through his retreat notes and letters. They are worthy to be remembered as words of encouragement for the faint-hearted. Here are a few. They were written at different times but have all the same spirit.

'I must buckle to in the life of faith.'

'To go amongst the heathen in the name of Christ should attract many souls. A glorious life is offered them, since the dangers are so great.'

'We must not trouble about health or life any more than a tree troubles about a leaf falling.'

'I must keep all my strength for God.'

'The weakness of human means is a source of strength.'

'One of the most urgent duties we owe to Our Lord is to be afraid of nothing.'

One might read through many books without coming across a line equal to these.

RÉNE BAZIN.

CONTENTS

	PAGE
PREFACE	V
INTRODUCTION	XV

PART I

THE TRAPPIST	3
MEDITATIONS ON THE GOSPEL	5

PART II

THE SERVANT OF THE POOR CLARES	37
RETREAT AT NAZARETH	37
EIGHT DAYS AT EPHRAIM	94
NOTES ON THE SPIRITUAL LIFE	129
LETTERS WRITTEN BETWEEN 1897 AND 1900	134

PART III

THE PRIEST, THE HERMIT IN THE SAHARA	155
RESOLUTIONS DURING THE ANNUAL RETREAT OF 1902	159
NOTES OF A RETREAT MADE IN 1904	163
SOME LETTERS, 1901–1916	166

INTRODUCTION

By Algar Thorold

CHARLES EUGÈNE DE FOUCAULD, the son of François-Édouard, Vicomte de Foucauld de Pont-Briand, was born at Strasbourg on September 15, 1856. The family was not of Alsatian origin. His father belonged to an ancient and noble stock of Périgord which had given to S. Louis a companion in arms who fell at Mansourah in defence of the King's life, and to a descendant of S. Louis a chamberlain who assisted at the coronation at Rheims of Charles VII by the side of S. Joan of Arc.

Bertrand the Crusader was not the only Foucauld to lose his life in the battles of the Church. On August 11, 1792, Armand de Foucauld, a Canon of Arles, who had refused to accept the civil constitution of the clergy, was arrested and imprisoned with other faithful ecclesiastics, including his own Archbishop, Mgr. du Nau, in the secularized Carmelite monastery at Paris. On September 2 they were all ordered into the garden. They knew the end was come. 'Let us thank God, gentlemen,' said the Archbishop, 'that he allows us to seal with our blood the faith we profess.'

The garden had filled suddenly with Redcaps armed with swords and pikes, and a moment later the martyrs were in Heaven.

As long as his mother lived, Charles breathed the atmosphere of normal Catholic childhood. But

INTRODUCTION

Mme de Foucauld died in the spring of 1864 and her husband only survived her five months; in consequence the two little orphans Charles and Marie were handed over to their maternal grandfather, M. Charles-Gabriel de Morlet, a retired colonel of Engineers, who at the time was close on seventy. The old man spoiled the boy. ' When he cries he reminds me of my daughter,' said he, and Charles' tears were not to be resisted. We are told that the future missionary had a violent temper and that the most amiable banter, that scourge of the young in the hands of their elders, drove him wild, wild with rage. In 1872 M. Morlet, who could not return to Strasbourg after the loss of the Provinces, took up his residence at Nancy. Here in due course Charles went to the Lycée. In later years he summed up his views on the religious results of the Lycée education as follows : ' I had no bad masters,—on the contrary all were very respectful (to religion) ; but even such as these do harm because they are neutral, and because youth needs to be instructed not by neutrals, but by believing and holy souls, and more than that by men who are learned in religious matters, capable of justifying their beliefs, and of inspiring young people with a firm confidence in the truth of their faith. . . . Let my experience be enough for the family, I beg of you.'[1]

At the age of fifteen Charles left Nancy for the Jesuit College in the Rue des Postes in Paris, where he was to be prepared for the military academy of S. Cyr. This is how he described his second year there to a friend :

' At the age of seventeen I began my second year at the Rue des Postes. I think I never was in a

[1] *Charles de Foucauld,* par René Bazin, p. 7.

INTRODUCTION

worse state of mind. In certain ways I have done more actual evil at other times, but then the ground produced good as evil fruit ; at seventeen I was all egotism, vanity and impiety. I was as it were mad with desire of evil . . . as to idleness it was such that they would not keep me at the Rue des Postes, and I have told you that in spite of the politeness employed so as not to wound my grandfather, I looked upon my departure as an expulsion, an expulsion of which idleness, was not the only motive . . . of faith not a trace remained in my soul.'[1]

And on another occasion he mentions that for ten years he did not believe in God.

We are apt to think that Saints must deliberately darken the colours in which they portray their pre-conversion days. Certainly they paint themselves more blackly than we in their places should. Yet the balance of error may not be on their side. They may see things more truly than we do. Be this as it may, we cannot doubt from his own words that Charles de Foucauld passed his first youth far from God. It was not until he was on the point of completing his thirtieth year in 1886 that he was touched by Grace. He had returned early in the year from his second geographical expedition in Africa and had settled down in Paris to prepare his great book, *Reconnaissance au Maroc*. In Paris he found numerous relatives : the Comtesse Armand de Foucauld, his father's sister, Inez, now Mme de Moitessier, and her two daughters, the Comtesse de Flavigny and the Vicomtesse de Bondy. Mme de Moitessier received a good deal in her fine hotel at the corner of Boulevard Malesherbes, and the tone of her *salon* was definitely Christian. Her husband's nephew, Louis Buffet, the youngest of Ministers,

[1] Bazin, op. cit., p. 9.

INTRODUCTION

Estancelin, the Duc de Broglie, were among her intimates. It was at her table that Charles met the servant of God to whom the work of his conversion had been entrusted, the Abbé Huvelin. This great man, who retained all his life the relatively humble position of Vicaire of the Church of S. Augustin, was an exquisitely cultivated humanist, a fine Greek scholar, a wit, and above all, a saint. In a letter to *The Times Literary Supplement* of May 25, 1922, Baron Friedrich Von Hügel refers parenthetically to ' the grandly tonic influence of Abbé Huvelin, that truly masculine saint who won and trained so many a soul,' and adds : ' *There* sanctity stood before me in the flesh and this as the deepest effect and reason of the Catholic Church.'

The Abbé Huvelin was sitting one morning in his confessional when a young man presented himself saying : ' M. l'Abbé, I have no faith, I come to ask for instruction.' It was Charles de Foucauld. The mysterious work of Grace had been going on for some time in his soul. He had been profoundly impressed in Morocco by the spectacle of the Arabs at prayer. That mysterious invocation of God repeated five times a day had gradually brought him to feel that he lacked something which the followers of the Prophet possessed. The pinchbeck gaiety of the French colony had come to ring very false against that almost infinite background of the desert, and the waste and hollow places of his own soul began to reveal themselves to him. Then the contact on his return to France with an atmosphere at once intellectual and Catholic in his family circle must have still further prepared his soul for the increasing influence of Grace. But the decisive stroke of that influence came from the personality of Huvelin. With true apostolic intuition the Abbé

INTRODUCTION

saw at once the state of mind of Foucauld, and bade him kneel down to make his confession, assuring him that he would believe when he had done so. After he had given his new penitent absolution he sent him straight to the Holy Table.

Foucauld did not talk much about his conversion. When his book was finished he made a pilgrimage to the Holy Land. On his return he made several retreats and in the early days of 1890 retired to the Trappe of Notre Dame des Neiges in the department of Lozère.

Up to the present Charles de Foucauld had followed what may be called the classic path of the great penitent, but now little by little his extraordinary personal vocation was to be revealed to him. He was not to stay at La Trappe. He made his profession in due course and became the edification of his brethren both at Notre Dame des Neiges and at Akbès in Syria, a small and very poor house of the Order, where he was sent at his own request. He was tormented by a desire growing ever more and more imperative for a life of greater solitude and abjection than any religious order could give him. His superiors after sending him to Rome for a three years' course of study, gave the necessary dispensations, and in 1897 he left Brindisi for the Holy Land once more. Here he became gardener and 'odd man' to the Poor Clares at Nazareth, and his life became more and more 'hid with Christ in God.' After three years of this hermit's life at Nazareth and Jerusalem, the Abbé Huvelin felt that the time was come when this amazing concentration and purification of soul ought to bear fruit and diffuse its benefits more widely and urged him to be ordained. So he returned to France and Notre Dame des Neiges, and there received the

INTRODUCTION

Priesthood in the summer of 1901. After a short visit to the Trappist monastery of Staoüeli and the French garrison at the advance post of Taghit he settled down at Béni-Abbès, an oasis in the Sahara. From here he moved to Tamanrasset in the Hoggar, where he remained until his death on December 1, 1916, at the hands of the savage Senoussi. It was his wish to found an order of apostolic hermits who should combine the contemplative life with the evangelization of the Mahomedan Tuaregs. Humanly speaking, this enterprise was a complete failure. From time to time a companion joined him, but none could persevere in the appalling austerity of life which he practised, and converts also failed him.

Charles de Foucauld from the moment when he first heard the call of Jesus Christ followed it with complete renunciation and simplicity. Seldom in the annals of sanctity has there been so complete a self-annihilation, so simple and naïf a love of the Cross. The writings which follow give the sublime explanation of this in so far as it can be given in words.

ALGAR THOROLD.

PART I

MEDITATIONS OF A HERMIT

THE TRAPPIST

NINE years after his conversion, January 16, 1890, Charles de Foucauld entered at the Trappist Monastery of Notre Dame des Neiges at Ardèche. He had begged that after six months there as a novice he might be sent to the poorest and most distant of their monasteries in Asia Minor. He left for the monastery of Béni-Abbès in Syria on June 17, 1890, and there he stayed until February 1897.

The following letters are taken from amongst his correspondence. They are signed ' Brother Marie-Albert ' and are written from both monasteries :

To a Trappist

TRAPPIST MONASTERY,
NOTRE DAME DU SACRÉ-COEUR,
SYRIA.
August 18, 1891.

How can one pity anyone who is doing the will of Our Lord ? Is there anything sweeter on earth than to do the will of him one loves ? And if it gives one some trouble to carry it out, the sweetness is all the greater.

MEDITATIONS OF A HERMIT

To a Trappist

February 7, 1891.

Our repose is to rejoice in the infinite happiness of God and, on a lower scale, in our own crosses and to desire still more of them, for in them we have the privilege of imitating him and proving our love, and there is nothing dearer to the heart that loves. We shall never lack either this happiness, nor God nor the Cross.

To a friend (on his birthday)

August 15, 1891.

All anniversaries seem to speak of our return to Eternity, all seem to cry out that Our Lord will not for ever be hidden from his poor children, and a birthday speaks more clearly of Heaven than anything. It is good to tell oneself when one is (as I so often am) horribly cold, lukewarm and full of distractions before the Blessed Sacrament that the day will come at last when Our Lord that we long so to love will appear in all his beauty, and that then we shall really love him. It is good to feel the days are passing. Who knows how much more we have to live? Whether it is to be long or short, may Our Lord live in us so that all that remains of life may be his, all for him, all for the consoling of his Sacred Heart.

November 29, 1896.

When one loves one longs to be for ever in converse with him one loves, or at least to be always in his sight. Prayer is nothing else. This is what prayer is. Intimate intercourse with the Beloved. You look at him, you tell him of your love, you are happy at his feet, you tell him you will live and die there.

MEDITATIONS ON THE GOSPEL

MEDITATIONS ON THE GOSPEL
EXTRACTS

THE Meditations from which some extracts are here given are upon two subjects : Prayer and Faith. Charles de Foucauld wrote them during his Trappist period, most of them, it would seem, in the Trappist monastery of Akbés, in Asia Minor. The reader will see that he chooses from each Evangelist in turn, S. Matthew, S. Mark, S. Luke and S. John, those texts which speak of Faith and of the intercourse of the soul with God.

I

PRAYER

> S. Matthew iv, 10. Then Jesus saith to him : Begone, Satan ! For it is written : The Lord shalt thou adore, and him only shalt thou serve.

'Thou shalt adore the Lord thy God.' It is you who are speaking, my Lord and my God. This is the first word you have spoken about prayer that is mentioned in the Gospel ; it is also the most important, the foundation of prayer. To worship is to see oneself at your feet as a cypher, a nothing, like dust that is only fit to be under your feet, but dust that thinks, that loves, a dust that admires, that venerates, that loves passionately, that kisses and embraces your feet whilst they trample upon it, that dissolves in love and adoration before you.

This is my first duty before you, my Lord and

MEDITATIONS OF A HERMIT

my God, my Master, my Creator, my Saviour, my beloved God.

I make these simple meditations for the purpose of my own perfection and that of others. This double work of perfection I desire only because it is the best that I can do for your glory. So bless, my God, this little undertaking, this sweet task, which I do for your glory only and for the consolation of your Sacred Heart. Sacred Heart of Jesus, I place in you this work I do for you. Fill it with grace and let it be what you wish. Our Lady of Perpetual Succour, grant me your powerful help in this and in all my thoughts, my words and actions, and the grace to seek it at all times.

My mother S. Mary Magdalen, S. Joseph, S. John the Baptist, S. Peter, S. Paul, my good Angel, you Holy Women who crushed sweet ointment to embalm Our Lord, crush some sweetness from this work of mine, crush me too that I may spread a sweet fragrance before the feet of Our Lord.

> S. Matthew v, 44. But I say to you: Love your enemies: do good to them that hate you: and pray for them that persecute and calumniate you.

We are to pray for our persecutors and our enemies. We must carry out this command carefully, with scrupulous and loving care. To make sure not to omit it we should fix some special prayer to say every day for our persecutors and our enemies. When our Beloved has let a command fall from his lips the least we can do is to gather it up and carry it out with eagerness and love and as perfectly as we can.

MEDITATIONS ON THE GOSPEL

> S. Matthew vi, 6. But thou when thou shalt pray, enter into thy chamber and, having shut the door, pray to thy Father in secret : and thy Father who seeth in secret will repay thee.

Here Our Lord gives us the precept of solitary prayer. We are to shut ourselves into our chamber and pray in solitude to our Father who sees our secret thoughts. So, besides our cherished prayer before the Blessed Sacrament, besides the prayers in common with others when Our Lord is in the midst of us gathered together in prayer, let us love to practise solitary and secret prayer, prayer in which no one sees us but our Heavenly Father, in which we are absolutely alone with him, when no one knows we are praying. What sweet intimacy to open our hearts freely, unseen by others, at the knees of our Father.

> S. Matthew vii, 8. For every one that asketh receiveth ; and he that seeketh, findeth ; and to him that knocketh, it shall be opened.

How earnestly we ought to pray for the glory of God, and for our own and our neighbour's sanctification, since we are absolutely certain of obtaining it. It surely is natural that he who loved enough to suffer so much for us should love us enough to grant us our desires. Ours is a great responsibility. If we do not pray we are responsible for all the good we might have done through prayer and have not done. What a terrible responsibility ! But how good Our Lord is to share his power

MEDITATIONS OF A HERMIT

with us, as it were, by setting such value upon our prayers.

> S. Matthew ix, 22. But Jesus turning and seeing her said: Be of good heart, daughter. Thy faith hath made thee whole. And the woman was made whole from that hour.

We see here that what Our Lord commends above everything else in prayer is Faith. He reminds us of it perpetually. Why? (1) Because it is what we most lack. (2) Because without it not only may our prayer not be acceptable to God, but it is actually injurious. I see only too well by my own experience how greatly we lack Faith. I am wanting in Faith for two reasons, first because I keep my eyes too much on myself and not enough upon God; I look too much at my own unworthiness instead of fixing them upon his goodness, his love, his Sacred Heart open to receive me. And secondly because I formulate my petition in too human a manner. I see all the difficulties presented by the graces I ask for and the impossibility for human nature to attain to them; I see the obstacles to their attainment, instead of keeping always before my eyes the power of God to which everything is easy. We should always keep our eyes fixed on the immense love God has for us, that love which made him endure such sufferings for each one of us, and which makes it so sweet and pleasant and natural to him to give us the greatest blessings. The greater the grace he gives the sweeter it is to him to give it, for such is the nature of love. It is infinitely easy to him to do things for us that seem to us impossibly difficult.

MEDITATIONS ON THE GOSPEL

> S. Matthew xiv, 23. And having dismissed the multitude he went into a mountain alone to pray. And when it was evening, he was there alone.

Our Lord prays alone and prays at night. It is his habit. Again and again the Gospel tells us that 'he went away alone by night to pray.' Let us love and cherish and practise this solitary nightly prayer of which he sets us an example. It is very sweet to be alone in intercourse with one one loves, with silence and peace and darkness all round. How sweet to speak alone with God at such times. These hours of unspeakable happiness and blessedness made S. Antony find the night too short. Whilst everything sleeps, drowned in silence and darkness, I live at the feet of God unfolding my soul to his love, telling him that I love him, and he replying that I will never love him, however great may be my love, as much as he cherishes me. What happiness to be allowed to spend these nights with God. Let me feel as I ought the value of such moments. Let me '*delectare in Domino.*' Let me, following your example, feel these hours of solitude and prayer by night to be more precious, more reposeful, more serene and more cherished than any others.

Teach me to prolong these hours in which I watch alone at your feet. Everything sleeps, no one knows of my happiness nor shares it. I rejoice through the solitude of the night in your presence, O my God. If these blessed solitary vigils could only consume my whole night how happy I should be. Many saints have had this joy. I know I do

MEDITATIONS OF A HERMIT

not deserve it, but I deserve no favours though you have given me so many, and I know so well how you love me. My God, if, as I believe, it is your will, give me this grace; I ask it by all the graces you have already given me, and for the sake of your Sacred Heart. Amen.

Our Lady of Perpetual Succour, you whom I have never invoked in vain, obtain for me this blessing and stretch out your hand to me to prevent me from sleeping as I so often do, alas! when I am at the feet of Our Lord. And may he invite me to pray with him to pass the hours in intercourse with him.

> S. Matthew xvii, 19. Jesus said to them: if you have faith as a grain of mustard seed, you shall say to this mountain, 'Remove from hence, and it shall remove': and nothing shall be impossible to you.

We can do anything by prayer. If our prayers are not answered it is either because we are wanting in faith, or because we have not prayed enough, or else that it would be bad for us if our request were granted, or perhaps God gives us something better than what we ask. But never do we not get what we ask because it is too difficult to get. We need never hesitate to ask God for the most difficult things, such as the conversion of great sinners or of whole nations. The more difficult things are to grant the more we must ask for them, believing that God loves us passionately. But we must ask with Faith, constantly, instantly, willingly, and with great love. We may be sure that if we ask thus and with enough persistence we shall be answered and be given the grace we ask or something even better.

Let us then ask bravely from God things that seem impossibilities, if they are for his glory. And the more they seem, humanly, to be impossible of attainment the more his Sacred Heart will grant them. For it is sweet to the Sacred Heart to do the impossible for those he loves. And how much he loves us !

> S. Matthew xvii, 20. This kind is not cast out save by prayer and fasting.

Not only by special prayer and fastings, but by a *life* of prayer and fasting. If we would resist the temptations of the devil we must lead a life of prayer and fasting. These are the two weapons that Our Lord shews us. To make our life a life of prayer two things are necessary ; first it must contain a long time every day given up entirely to prayer ; secondly, during the hours given up to other occupations, we must remain united to God, keeping ourselves always in his presence and constantly turning our hearts to thoughts of him.

> S. Matthew xviii, 14. It is not the will of your Father who is in Heaven, that one of these little ones should perish.

Our Lord came to find that which was lost. He leaves the sheep that are safe in the fold and sets out to look for the one that has wandered away. Let us do like him, and since our prayers are a force and since they are certain to obtain what they ask, we should fly to the rescue of sinners. Through our prayers we can do the work for which our

MEDITATIONS OF A HERMIT

Divine Spouse came on earth. Those of us who are not already dedicated to the apostolic life should pray for the conversion of sinners, because prayer is almost the only means, though it is a powerful and far-reaching means, of doing them good and helping the Divine Spouse in his work, of saving his children, of drawing out of mortal peril those souls that he loves so passionately and which he has told us in the Gospels to love as he loves them. Even if we are dedicated to an active apostolate it will never bear fruit unless we pray for those we hope to convert, for Our Lord gives only to him who asks, opens only to him who knocks. We need the grace of God to put good words into our mouths, good inspirations into our hearts, and good will into the hearts of those who hear us, and we must ask for this grace in order to receive it. So whatever may be our life, let us pray a great deal for the conversion of sinners since it is above all for them that Our Lord worked and suffered and prayed. Let us pray every day with all our hearts for the salvation and sanctification of all those wandering souls that were so much beloved by Our Lord, that they may not perish, but be happy. Let us pray every day for them, at great length and with all our hearts, so that the Heart of Jesus may be consoled by their conversion and rejoiced by their salvation.

> S. Matthew xxi, 13. My house shall be called the house of prayer ; but you have made it a den of thieves.

This shows us the infinite respect we should have for all churches. We must be recollected and respectful in them, and if in the time of Our Lord recollectedness was obligatory how much more now, when Our Lord dwells in our Tabernacles.

Our Lord's words mean something besides. They apply to our souls. Our soul also is a house of prayer. Prayer should rise unceasingly from it to Heaven, like the smoke of incense. But how often distractions of worldly thoughts, thoughts that are not at all for the glory of God, even bad thoughts, break in, and fill our souls with noise and disturbance and filth, and turn them into dens of thieves.

Let us try with all our strength to occupy our minds only with God or with that which he gives us to do for his service. Even whilst doing our tasks for him we must keep our eyes fixed constantly on him, never detaching our heart from him, only keeping our attention on our tasks as much as is right and necessary, never our hearts. God must be the King of our minds, the Lord of our minds, so that the thought of him never leaves us, and we speak, think and act always either for him or guided by love of him. Let our souls be thus a house of prayer and not a den of thieves. Let no stranger enter in, no profanity even in passing. Let it always be occupied with its Beloved. When one loves one never loses sight of that which one loves.

> S. Matthew xxi, 16. And the children cried in the Temple, 'Hosanna to the son of David.'

Our Lord commends the children who cried 'Hosanna to the son of David.' He approves them. He wishes to be praised. It is not enough to thank him, to ask pardon and pray to him for graces. Those three words 'thanks, pardon and help' are indispensable and should always be in our hearts and on our lips. But they are not enough if we would pray rightly. We must praise him too. To praise God is to express one's admiration and one's love, for love is inseparable from unstinted admiration. To praise God is to melt at his feet with words of love and admiration, to tell him unceasingly that he is infinitely perfect, infinitely loved and lovable, that his beauty and our admiration and our love are immeasurable ; to tell him endlessly, make untiringly the sweet declaration, that he is Beauty and that we love him.

Praise is an essential part of love. It is an all-essential part of our service of God. This is easy to see. But there is a second reason for which we owe God praise. This is that, on his side, it is an incomparable favour to allow us to speak to him. For us to allow someone to repeat to us constantly in every possible form of speech, that he loves us, would be the greatest favour we can shew him. It would shew that his love is pleasing to us, almost that we love him too. God lets us stay at his feet whispering perpetually our words of love and admiration. What joy, what grace, what goodness. But how ungrateful we shall be if we despise this great favour and make no use of it. God not only allows us this great favour, but he commands it. He commands us to tell him that we love him and adore him, and if we do not respond to this sweet and precious invitation we shew ingratitude and unworthiness and discourtesy and unnaturalness. My Lord and my God, teach me to find all my joy in praising you, in repeating to you unceasingly that I love you infinitely and that you are infinitely adorable. '*Delectare in Domino et dabit tibi petitiones tuas*' were your words. Teach me to

MEDITATIONS ON THE GOSPEL

delight in you and your infinite beauty and in the incessant outpouring of praise at your feet.

S. Mary Magdalen, obtain for me the grace to praise Our Lord, our common Master, as he would have me praise him.

> S. Matthew xxvi, 36. Sit you here, till I go yonder and pray.

What is Our Lord doing in this last hour before his arrest, before his Passion begins? He goes away alone to pray. So we, when we have a severe trial to undergo, or some danger or some suffering to face, go aside to pray in solitude, and so pass the last hours that separate us from our trial.[1] Let us do this in every serious event in our lives. Let us prepare for it, gather strength, light, grace, to behave well, by praying and praying alone during the last hours before our trial.

> S. Matthew xxvi, 38. Stay you here and watch with me.

Was it only to his three apostles that Our Lord said this?

No, it was to all of us that he said it, to us whom he loves and who are in his mind during his Agony, to all of us whose faithful companionship is comforting to him during these sorrowful hours. Let us then be faithful to this practice of 'watching with him,' helping him, consoling him, sympathizing with him with all our hearts in his Agony. To watch with Our Lord on Thursday nights should be our faithful practice all our lives. May we never miss it for the sake of the Divine Heart of Our Lord. He formally asks it of us in the words spoken to his

---

[1] It was in such solitary prayer that Charles de Foucauld passed the last hours that preceded his violent death.

MEDITATIONS OF A HERMIT

apostles. Shall we refuse him? O Holy Virgin, O my Guardian Angel, help me, I pray you, that I may never be so unworthy, so hateful as to refuse him this.

S. Matthew xxvi, 39. He fell upon his face praying.

Our Lord knelt to pray, so let us imitate him and pray on our knees, in a posture of humility, supplication and penance. It becomes us to pray thus; moreover, it is the loving attitude. What is the attitude of love if it is not to kneel at the feet of the Beloved. We need not be afraid of sitting in his presence like Mary Magdalen, or of standing, but it is best to kneel as he knelt, in a spirit of humility and penance, but above all of love.

S. Matthew xxvi, 39. My Father, if it be possible, let this chalice pass from me. Nevertheless, not as I will but as thou wilt.

Our Lord shews us how to pray. We should first ask God all we need simply, like a child who asks his father, and then we must add ' but not my will but Thine be done.'

S. Matthew xxvi, 40. What? Could you not watch one hour with me?

You do not say this only to your apostles, O my Lord, but to all of us who might watch with you, keep you company in the sadness of your Sacred Heart, console you with faithful love. But we do not do it. We go off to sleep; we lack courage and love, forgetting how precious is a vigil with you, forgetting that to watch at your feet is such an infinite privilege that even the Saints and Angels are unworthy of it, forgetting to rejoice in your presence as one rejoices in the presence of some much loved creature, and to long to console you with passionate love. If our longing was great and passionate enough to console and comfort you, we should never give in to this low, bestial temptation to sleep. If we felt, as we should, the infinite peace of praying at your feet, should we not always be there praying with you, not noticing how the time goes, fearing only one thing in our happiness—its end ? Alas ! my God, I am one of these low, base creatures, for how often do I fall asleep at your very feet when I should be praying with you. Forgive me, forgive me. Help me, my God, never to fall into this hateful coldness and infidelity. Many times have I fallen, I hate my fault, it is horrible to me. I ask your pardon, my God, with all my soul.

> The Gospel of S. Mark i, 35. And rising very early, going out, he went into a desert place : and there he prayed.

Let us do what Our Lord did and rise early in the morning, whilst everything is at rest in silence and darkness, when sleep envelops everything in torpor, in profound quiet. Let us rise and watch with God, lifting our hearts to him, laying our souls at his feet, and at this early hour when intercourse is so secret and so sweet let us fall at his feet and enjoy converse with Our Creator. How good he is to let us come to his feet whilst all is sleeping. How good he is to allow his poor creatures this intercourse with his Sovereign Majesty, with his ineffable beauty. Our whole soul should rejoice in these happy moments, privileged beyond words, privilege of which neither man, nor angel, nor saint is worthy. Let us every day and all our lives do this of which Our Lord sets us an example and which should be our greatest happiness, divine happiness. Let us rise early in the morning, before daybreak, and, whilst all else is sleeping in silence and shadow, let us begin both our day and our prayers. Before our working day begins let us pass long hours praying at the feet of Our Lord. Let us not only pray part of the night before the day breaks, but pray alone, forgotten by all in that solitude. If prayer in common is enjoined by him, so is secret and solitary prayer, and in both we have his example. Let us follow both precepts and both examples.

> S. Mark vii, 29. And she besought him that he would cast forth the devil out of her daughter.
> Jesus said to her : Suffer first the children to be filled : for it is not good to take the bread of the children and cast it to the dogs.
> But she answered and said to him : Yea, Lord ; for the whelps also eat under the table of the crumbs of the children.
> And he said to her : For this saying, go thy way. The devil is gone out of thy daughter.

Our Lord commends aloud the prayer of the Phœnician woman, and in this makes her a model for us all. What is to be seen first of all in this

MEDITATIONS ON THE GOSPEL

prayer? Faith, humility, persistence, brevity, simplicity. Her persistence is such that no rebuff can move her from her purpose. Let us be like her, let us be simple and brief in our prayers, so humble that we are not indignant at being compared to the dogs, and so persistent and so faithful that no difficulty or dryness or delay in the granting of our prayer can change or discourage us.

> S. Mark xiv, 38. Watch ye : and pray that you enter not into temptation. The spirit indeed is willing, but the flesh is weak.

We need two things to resist temptation. Firstly, long hours of prayer every day with unchanging regularity. Secondly, constant prayer all the rest of one's time. That is to say, that during the many occupations that fill the day our minds must be constantly fixed on God, and our eyes always turned towards him either by using ejaculatory prayer or simply by turning our thoughts to him. It matters little what means we use, so long as the soul gazes on her Beloved. If we are working at anything in the presence of one we love we cannot forget his presence for a moment. Our eyes are on him constantly and the time passes quickly and happily. It should be the same with Our Lord, the Divine Spouse of our souls. Perpetual prayer throughout the day will keep temptations from our souls, the presence of Our Lord will drive them away and prevent their harming us. The hours given up entirely to prayer will give us the strength, with God's grace, to keep ourselves in his presence through the rest of the day and give up all our time to what is called ' perpetual prayer.'

MEDITATIONS OF A HERMIT

S. Mark xv, 34. Eloi, Eloi, lamma sabachthani?

These words teach us two things. First, that we must speak to God with perfect simplicity, telling him all our thoughts, even our complaints. We should express our joy, in gratitude give him thanks, in penitence ask his pardon, in our desires ask for fulfilment, in sorrow shew him our grief. Since our sufferings are allowed by him we may make our plaint to God as Our Lord did, but we should complain with all reverence, love, submission, unbounded and loving conformity to his will. Such his only Son shewed for him, and we his children owe the same to him, so loaded with graces as we are by this infinitely good and lovable Father. Second, Our Lord uses two words of Holy Scriptures in speaking to his Father. We should use words of Scripture too since they come from the Holy Spirit, use them in our longer prayers, as the ancient Jews used to do and as the Church does, the spouse of Christ. We can use them too as ejaculatory prayers as Our Lord does here. He gives us this example in several places to shew us that it was a habit with him, and that we should make it our habit. He uses words of Scripture to express the cry of his soul at those most solemn moments, in the temptation in the wilderness and on the Cross. Two words of the Psalms are his last before his death. It is very clear we should follow this example of his. For the words of Scripture inspired by God are surely worth more than any words of ours. What better offering can we make to God, next to the Body of his Son, than the words his Sacred Heart has poured from Heaven on to earth, his own holy words fallen from his own lips.

MEDITATIONS ON THE GOSPEL

> S. Luke x, 42. Mary hath chosen the best part, which shall not be taken away from her.

The 'better part' is the Contemplative Life, the life that is completely detached from material things, and is only concerned with the contemplation of Our Lord. In this life the spirit no longer is occupied with earthly things, but is immersed in the thought of God, contemplates him, listens to him, speaks to him unceasingly in a constant sense of his presence and a prayer which, though it may vary at different hours of the day, never ceases.

Though Mary Magdalen lives like others outwardly, whatever she does, her eyes, her heart, her thoughts, are always given to Our Lord. In him consists her life. This is the contemplative life, the life of passionate love, of adoring love. This is the 'better part,' the 'part' of the Blessed Virgin and S. Joseph at Nazareth, the 'part' of the Blessed Virgin all through her life, of S. John the Baptist in the desert, the 'part' of Mary Magdalen at Bethany, in Galilee, in Judea, in Provence. May it be our own 'part.' Let us imitate our Blessed Mother, S. Mary Magdalen, the passionate adorer of Christ.

> S. Luke xv, 10. There will be joy before the angels of God over one sinner doing penance.

There will be joy, and therefore thanksgiving, for all good comes from God. Thanksgiving should have a large place in our prayers, for the goodness of God precedes all our acts and envelops every instant of our lives. There is not a moment in our

MEDITATIONS OF A HERMIT

existence in which we do not receive such a multitude of blessings that all Eternity would not be long enough in which to thank for each one of them. When we are before the Blessed Sacrament let our first words be ' Thanks, thanks that I am at your feet. How blessed to be here!' And whenever we pray, ' Thanks and again thanks that you let me speak to you, contemplate you, converse with you, my Lord and my God, my Beloved, my Joy, my Life.' We should not only give thanks for ourselves, but for all men. They are our brothers, and so your children, my God, and therefore to be loved by me. Thanks for all the souls in Purgatory, for all the Saints, and for those Saints especially for whom you have given me a special love. Thanks for the most Holy Virgin. Thanks above all for yourself, my Lord and my God, whose glory and blessedness are my strong and sure joy, an endless source of joy that nothing can take from me.

S. Luke xix, 40. If these shall hold their peace, the stones will cry out.

How right that you should be praised, Lord Jesus ! It is indispensable that praise should be a large part of our worship. Our prayers must be full of praise and adoration. It is not enough to use the three invocations : thanks, pardon, help. These invocations must ever be preceded by worship. ' I adore thee,' that is : ' I love thee, I praise thee, thou art infinitely lovely.' With all my strength I proclaim it (and I long to proclaim it so that your glory may be served) to thy honour and glory, and though I am nothing I can serve to praise thy beauty, though to praise thee rightly is infinitely impossible.

MEDITATIONS ON THE GOSPEL

Thou alone art fit to praise thyself, O God. So I unite myself to you, O Jesus, my Lord, to praise your Father. I unite myself to you, O Holy Spirit, from whom the impulse comes, to praise Jesus Christ. And I unite myself to you, O Father and Son, to praise the Holy Ghost my God, co-equal with both.

Thus adoration and praise must be in all our prayers. When we address God it should be our first movement of respect and love.

> S. Luke xxii, 43. And being in an agony, he prayed the longer.

Pray to Our Lord to make you follow his example. The more you suffer, the more you are tempted, the more you need to pray; prayer now alone can strengthen you with help and consolation. Let not pain and fierce temptation paralyse your prayer. The devil does all he can to prevent you praying at these times. But rather than give in to weak human nature which absorbs the soul in its pain so that it sees nothing else for the time, turn your eyes to Our Lord and speak to him standing so near. He is with you, looking on you lovingly, listening for your words. He tells you to speak, that he is there to hear you, that he loves you and you have not a word to say to him, no look to give him. What ingratitude! Look at him, speak to him without ceasing, as you do to those you love and as Our Lord did here on earth with his Father. The deeper your agony, the deeper you must bury yourself in the Heart of your Beloved, and cling to his side with ceaseless prayer. My God, give me this grace that I may follow your example in this duty so pressing and so sweet.

MEDITATIONS OF A HERMIT

> S. Luke xxiii, 46. Father, into thy hands I commend my spirit.

This is the last prayer of Our Master, our Beloved. May it be ours. And not only ours at our last moments, but at all times. ' My Father, I commend myself to you, I give myself to you, I leave myself in your hands. My Father, do with me as you wish. Whatever you do with me, I thank you, I accept everything. I am ready for anything. I thank you always. So long as your will is done in me and in all creatures, I have no other wish, my God. I put my soul into your hands, giving it to you, my God, with all my heart's love, which makes me crave to abandon myself to you without reserve, with utter confidence. For are you not my Father?

> S. John iii, 29. The friend of the bride-groom, who standeth and heareth him, rejoiceth with joy because of the bride-groom's voice.

Surely I should repeat these words, my God, my Lord Jesus, every time I hear an inspired text like the Psalms, the Gospels, the Pater, the Ave, or any other words out of the Scriptures. It is the voice of the Holy Ghost that I hear or read. So when I read these words of S. John I like to add with him, ' This my joy is fulfilled.' My joy is fulfilled every time I hear or read or recite any passage, however short, that contains God's words, the words of the Beloved, of the Spouse so passionately beloved. This joy, the transport of happiness that the voice of my Beloved gives me, is with me when I say the Divine Office, or the Rosary, and read the Holy

MEDITATIONS ON THE GOSPEL

Scriptures. With what love, devotion, veneration one adores the words of a loved one. Let me then embrace and cherish adoringly the words of my Beloved.

> S. John xii, 27. Father, save me from this hour. But for this cause I came unto this hour. Father, glorify now thy Son.

This is another form of the prayer of Gethsemane, a simple cry to God of our human nature, human nature in great suffering and great need, but which then pulls itself together and cries: 'My God, what matters this or any other thing I may suffer.' All I care for is your glory. I ask only this and nothing else. Forget my first request. I made it to you as my Father, because in duty I should shew you my pressing need. But having shewn you my need, in all simplicity I only say over and over again how infinitely greater is my need, my desire, for your glory and honour. This is my true and only desire, and I pray you with all my soul to satisfy this desire. My Father, glorify yourself in me. My Father, glorify your Holy Name. My Lord Jesus, let me, a miserable creature, join with you in making this prayer. My God, my voice unites with the adorable voice of my Lord Jesus in saying 'Not my will but thine be done.' My only desire is for your glory; this is what I thirst for. My Father, do with me as you please, whatever it may be. My Father, may your name be glorified.

> S. John xv, 7. Ask whatever you will: and it shall be done unto you.

It shall be given to you, or else, as the Fathers

MEDITATIONS OF A HERMIT

have added, I will give you something better. Our Lord promises to answer all our prayers (if they are pure and free from sin ; anything else would be an insult to ask). That is to say, the thing he reserves to himself is to change the request into something better, to give us even more than we ask. O blessed reservation, worthy of your Sacred Heart, O Lord ! Divine reservation indeed by which you contrive to give even more than all we ask. How good you are and how blessed are we !

And what wisdom in your foresight ! For our ignorance is so great that with the best intentions we often ask for mean and harmful things, things that would do harm rather than good. But you, my God and my Father, settle all for us and give us only what is best for us.

> S. John xvii, 1. Father, the hour is come. Glorify thy Son, that thy Son may glorify thee.

This is the longest prayer of Our Lord's that is preserved for us in the Gospels (the prayer after the Last Supper). Let us study it in detail and imprint it upon our minds so as to make this prayer a model for our own. Let us consider two things in particular : the general character of the prayer and its matter in this verse quoted. Its *character* is confidence, abandonment ; its terms are great simplicity, tender familiarity. ' Father,' a son is speaking with tender, intimate confidence to his Father. Its *matter* is the glory of God ' that your Son may glorify you.' Note that the character and substance are both those of the first words of the Pater Noster. ' Our Father, hallowed be thy name.' Therefore this confidence and tender familiarity, this petition that comes first and above all others, that God may be glorified, should be the note of all our prayers and be their foundation and their principal theme.

> S. John xvii, 2–5. Thou hast given him power over all flesh, that he may give eternal life to all whom thou hast given him. Now this is eternal life : that they may know thee, the only true God, and Jesus Christ, whom thou hast sent.
> I have glorified thee on the earth ; I have finished the work which thou gavest me to do.
> And now glorify thou me, O Father, with thyself, with the glory which I had, before the world was, with thee.

The character of this prayer is still perfect confidence, simplicity, familiarity. Our Lord is ' thinking aloud ' at his Father's feet. The matter is that he prays for death, he prays for Heaven. Let us imitate him in this too. Our prayers should have this same note of filial confidence ; let us ' think aloud ' at Our Lord's feet, and let us pray often that our exile may end and that death may bring us nearer to him. Let us pray for it very fervently ; pray that we may see him, enjoy him, possess him, and love him perfectly, never more offend him. We should often pray God to take us away soon from this world where we offend him so often and love him so badly, and where we are separated from him, and beg him to take us to

MEDITATIONS OF A HERMIT

Heaven where we shall love him without offending him and shall be at his feet through all Eternity.

S. John xix, 30. It is consummated.

S. John here gives us the last words addressed by Our Lord to his Father. 'I have accomplished all that you have given me to do.' My God, let these be our words in our last hour ! Not in the same sense of perfect accomplishment—we are such poor human beings—but at least in the measure of our miserable capacity. To this end, O my God, I must pray you to shew me my task, and pray you to accomplish it, since all power comes from you alone. My Lord and my God, I pray you let me know your will clearly. And then give me the strength to carry it out faithfully to the end with gratitude and love. I seem to hear your answer, O my God. 'The attraction I have given you, its strength, its persistence, its beauty, shew you what I ask of you. But I grant this vocation on one condition, that you turn yourself altogether to me and set your feet on the Way of Perfection. I am still waiting and you still have not taken the first step forward, rather have you gone back than forward. Press onward on, turn to me : I have waited so long. My patience will not last for ever.' O my God, pardon me, pardon me for my coldness, my cowardliness, my wasted time, my pride, my love of my own will, forgive me my weakness and unfaithfulness, the confusion of my thoughts, my forgetfulness of your presence. Forgive, forgive my sins, all the faults of my life, and particularly those I have fallen into since my conversion : I thank you for your many graces. My Lord and my God, come to my aid, help me on whom you have showered your gifts so that I might be converted and let me use the gifts that you still offer me so that I may do whatever you ask of me, whatever, in your infinite goodness, you call me to do, I who am so unworthy. Turn my heart towards you, my God, for the sake of Our Lord Jesus Christ. You can ' of these stones raise up sons to Abraham.' You are all powerful over your creatures, you can do all things in me. Give me a right mind, give me the wisdom that you promise to all who ask for it. Convert my heart and let me glorify you to the utmost till my last breath and through all Eternity. I ask this in the name of Our Saviour Jesus Christ. Amen. Amen. Amen.

II

FAITH

S. Matthew viii, 26. And Jesus saith to them : Why are you fearful, O ye of little faith ?

One thing we owe to Our Lord is never to be afraid. To be afraid is doubly an injury to him. Firstly, it means that we forget him ; we forget he is with us and is all powerful ; secondly, it means that we are not conformed to his will ; for since all that happens is willed or permitted by him, we ought to rejoice in all that happens to us and feel neither anxiety nor fear. Let us then have the faith that banishes fear. Our Lord is at our side, with us, upholding us. Jesus, Our God, with his infinite love, who is all powerful and knows what is for our good, and who tells us to seek first the Kingdom

MEDITATIONS OF A HERMIT

of God and all the rest shall be added. Let us go straight ahead in this blessed company in the Way of Perfection, and let us be assured that nothing can happen to us but that from which we can draw the greatest possible good for his glory and our sanctification and that of others. All that happens to us is willed or allowed by him; therefore, rather than have the shadow of a fear we have only to say to him: 'Lord, whatever happens, blessed be thy Name,' and pray him to settle things not according to our ideas but always for his greater glory. We must never forget these two precepts: 'Jesus is with us.' 'All that happens is by the Will of God.'

> S. Matthew ix, 22. But Jesus, turning and seeing her, said: Be of good heart, daughter. Thy faith hath made thee whole. And the woman was made whole from that hour.

Faith is the virtue that Our Lord most often rewards and praises. Sometimes he praises love, as in the case of Mary Magdalen. Sometimes humility, but these are rare cases, and it is nearly always faith that earns his approval and reward. Why is this? No doubt because it is the most important of the virtues, if not the greatest, for it is the foundation of all the others, including charity, and it is the rarest of all. To have real faith, faith that inspires all one's actions, and faith in the supernatural which tears the mask from the world and sees God in everything, which makes all things possible, which takes all meaning out of such words as worry, peril, fear, which makes us pass through life calmly, peacefully, happily, like a child holding its mother's hand, which gives the soul perfect detachment from all material things, shewing it their emptiness and puerility; which gives to prayer the confidence of a child asking something he deserves from his father; a faith to which all is falsehood except to do the Will of God; a faith that makes all appear in a new light, so that we see men in the likeness of God making us love them and respect them as the counterfoils of our Beloved, and do them all the good we can. It will help us to regard all other living things as aids to the winning of Heaven, for we can always give God praise for them, or use them, or renounce them. Faith will shew us the greatness of God and our own littleness. It will make us undertake whatever is pleasing to God without hesitation or false shame or fear and without looking back. Ah! such faith is rare indeed. My God, give me this faith; my God, I believe, help thou my unbelief; my God, let me believe and love. I ask it in the name of Our Lord Jesus Christ.

S. Matthew xiv, 31. O thou of little faith, why didst thou doubt?

Our Lord asks great faith from us, and he is right. We owe him great faith. After Our Lord said 'Come' to him, Peter had no more fear and walked upon the waters. So that when Jesus has quite certainly called us to certain circumstances in life, given us a certain vocation, we need fear nothing, but should attack the most insurmountable obstacles without hesitation. If Jesus has said 'Come,' we have the grace to walk upon the waters. It may seem to us impossible, but Jesus overmasters the impossible. So we need three things: first, to call out to Our Lord very clearly, and then, when we have distinctly heard his 'Come' (without this summons we have not the right to throw ourselves into the waters—it would be presumptuous, imprudent and rash, and a risk to the life of the soul ; it would be sinful, even to mortal sin, for to risk the life of the soul is even graver than to risk the life of the body), once his 'Come' is heard by the soul (till that moment our duty is simply to pray and wait), we must hesitate no more but throw ourselves into the waters like S. Peter and, confident in the call that God has given, walk over the waves, without hesitation, without the least doubt or fear, sure that if we go forward in faith and confidence the path that Jesus calls to us to follow will become easy to us by the virtue of his call 'Come.' So let us walk with perfect faith in the way along which he calls us, for heaven and earth shall pass away but his words shall not pass.

S. Matthew xv, 28. O woman, great is thy faith. Be it done to thee as thou wilt.

Our Lord praises the Canaanite woman for persisting in prayer in spite of his refusals and for her faith in his power and goodness. It is because of this constancy that he grants her request. So when we pray with faith and persistence our prayers will be answered.

Our Lord is the same as in those days when he went about on the coasts of the Sea of Galilee. Man changes, but God does not change. He is exactly the same as he was then, in his divinity, his power, his goodness, his compassion for men, and he is still as ready as ever to give us what we ask. So therefore let us ask him.

MEDITATIONS ON THE GOSPEL

S. Matthew xvi, 8. Why do you think within yourselves, O ye of little faith, that you have no bread?

So Our Lord does not let his servants doubt that they will always have their daily bread in such measure as is good for their souls. He is right to forbid them all anxiety on this point. Right for two reasons, but, firstly, because he said : 'Seek first the Kingdom of God and all things shall be added unto you.' By these words Our Lord undertakes to give the necessaries of life to all those who become his disciples, and who embrace poverty in the religious life for the sake of following him, in so far as it is good for them, provided they really seek to serve him. For the religious to doubt or to be anxious about temporal things would be to lack faith in the promise of Jesus and so to offend him mortally.

Secondly, when a man loves, he thinks of one thing only : the beloved one. His only anxiety is to make the beloved happy, and to possess the beloved. He is unable to attach the least importance to anything else. When a man loves, one thing only exists for him ; the beloved. The rest of the world is nothing to him, it does not exist. In the heart that loves God can there be room for material doubts and anxieties?

S. Mark xi, 22–23–24. Have faith in God. All things whatsoever you ask when ye pray, believe that you shall receive : and they shall come unto you.

Again and again you repeat these words, O Lord,

MEDITATIONS OF A HERMIT

in all the Gospels and in the same terms. They must indeed be weighty for you to repeat them so insistently. Give me then grace that they may penetrate my mind and heart. All that I ask from you, provided I ask it with faith and confidence, that you will give, that I shall obtain. That is, of course, I must not ask anything that would be harmful, or something mean that, though it seems great in my eyes, is really much less than what you wish to give me. You are a Father, all powerful and infinitely wise and good and tender. You say to us as your children, so frail we are and hardly able to walk except with our hand in yours, ' all that you ask I will give you if only you ask with confidence.' And you do give it, so willingly and easily when our petitions are reasonable and in accord with your desires, and with the feelings that you like to see in our hearts and in conformity with all that you yourself desire, more ardently than we can ever do. If we ask you for dangerous playthings you refuse them in goodness for us, and you console us by giving us other things for our good. If we ask you to put us where it would be dangerous for us to be you do not give us what is not for our good, but you give us something really for our welfare, something that we would ask for ourselves if our eyes were open. You take us by the hand and lead us, not there where we would wish to go, but there where it is best for us to be.

PART II

THE SERVANT OF THE POOR CLARES

DURING the six years that he lived at La Trappe his vocation was assured. This was the most remarkable vocation of modern times, and it was to lead Charles de Foucauld into the severest solitude the world can offer. At the beginning of 1897, the time came for him to renew his Trappist vows. With the approval of his superiors he embraced his special vocation, left La Trappe, and offered himself as servant, gardener, messenger, to a convent of Poor Clares at Nazareth. In this manner he passed about three years from 1897–1900.

A RETREAT MADE AT NAZARETH
November 5–15, 1897.

Charles de Foucauld was living at this time in a wooden hut, a sort of shed roofed with tiles, built up against the walls of the Poor Clares' cloister, which had been used for keeping the garden tools. In this retreat he made his meditations, either in his cell or else in the chapel of the Convent before the exposed Host. Hence the allusion to the silence of the country, or the presence of Our Lord in the Blessed Sacrament.

THE OBJECT OF THE RETREAT

My Lord and my God, present here and in me and around me, I adore you with all my soul; I thank you for your infinite mercies. Pardon my constant faithlessness. Come to my aid that I may console you with all my power every moment of my life.

The aim of this retreat is to know your will better, to do it better and so work for your good. Give it your blessing, my God. I make it for your sake; not only for myself, but for you; not for others, but for you. I am bound to love myself and to love others, but for your sake only. We are secondary, but you come first and above all, you who alone have Being. Grant, O my God, that I may make this retreat as well as possible, in you, by you and for you, and that it may make me to know you and love you. To know your will and do it, and do all to console your Sacred Heart, this is the one thing I desire.

GOD —
HIS PERFECTION. HIS PRESENCE

My God, how good you are! This morning I was in my cell, where I pass such happy hours at night in silent converse with you, whilst all the earth is sleeping. There at your feet I adored you, telling you of my love, whilst all was buried in darkness, silence and sleep. But now, oh, happy grace, I am before the Blessed Sacrament and the Blessed Sacrament exposed. What happiness! I am so near to you, so close to you, O my God. Let me serve you here in your presence as I ought, give me such thoughts and words as I should have in you, by you and for you.

Thank you, my God, for letting me begin my retreat thus on a day of Exposition of the Blessed Sacrament. You give me all the graces. Thank you, thank you, my God, thank you for your graces because they are so sweet, thank you because I

RETREAT AT NAZARETH

know how much I need them and how much need of special help I have for my special weakness, cowardice and lukewarmness. You give your help, not in proportion to our merit, but to our needs. You came for the sick and not for the healthy. How true I feel this is. I feel your love as you hold me to your Sacred Heart, my Beloved Jesus, my God, my Master, but I feel, too, the need I have of your tenderness, and of your caress because of my infinite weakness.

In this retreat you wish me first of all to consider you. You, God, and you, Jesus, God and Man. Then to consider what you ask of me, that is to say my duty, and that again is to say my own life, my own self; for my whole life, my whole self should be nothing else but the accomplishment of my duty and of your will. Let it be so, let there never be any divergence between *me myself and the accomplishment of your Will*. O my God, let these two ever be united, in you, by you, for you. Amen.

I must consider God. I, a worm, am to lift my eyes to you, the Infinite. How is this possible? And yet it is possible, for you tell us that it is a duty. We alone of all created things, can and should raise our hearts to you; rising through material beauty to the beauty of the soul and of spiritual things. Rising step by step upon the ladder of created things we can attain to the perception of the perfect Mind, adding perfections, eliminating imperfections, and carrying the thought of perfect beauty on to that excelling perfection, till we finally attain to the idea of what you are, my Father, my Creator, my Father, my Beloved; you who are there, a few feet from me, under the appearance of the Host, you are the Supreme Beauty. All created beauty, all beauty of Nature, the beauty of the sunset, of the

MEDITATIONS OF A HERMIT

sea lying like a mirror beneath the blue sky, of the dark forest, of the garden of flowers, of the mountains and the great spaces of the desert, of the snow and the ice, the beauty of a rare soul reflected in a beautiful face, all these beauties are but the palest reflection of yours, my God. All that has ever charmed my eyes in this world is but the poorest, the humblest reflection of your infinite Beauty.

O my God, give me the grace to see nothing else but you, nothing but you in all created things ; never to be arrested by them, never to see the natural or spiritual beauty that is in them as being born of themselves, but only as being part of you.

Let my mind pierce through the veil and not rest on these poor things made of mingled life and nothingness, ruinous, decaying, empty. But, through all the Being that I see in created things, pass at once beyond their appearance and beyond their poor consistency and perceive the Essential Being to which all beings belong and which has cast a fragment of itself into these created things in which we take pleasure. If this fragment seems to us so lovely, how much more lovely is the perfect Being who has thrown it to us as alms, like a penny thrown to a beggar. My God, give me that Grace you gave to S. Teresa, never to attribute to created things themselves the spiritual or material beauty that may be in them, or to rest in them, for these come not from themselves, but from the Sovereign Being. To rest in them would be ungrateful, discourteous, an abuse of confidence, for God gave this beauty to created things that he may shew himself to me, and my pleasure in them, to rouse my gratitude, through them, for his goodness, my love for his Beauty, and make me climb to his throne and there establish the life of my soul in adoration, in wondering contemplation and gratitude. So my conversation will be in Heaven, since earthly sights can only let me guess at your beauty and your tender love.

And he is near me, this perfect Being, who is All Being, who is the only true Being, who is all Beauty, goodness, wisdom, love, knowledge, intelligence. Those creatures in whom I admire a reflection of his perfections, on whom there falls a little ray of the infinite sunshine, are outside me, far removed from me, distant and separate, whilst you, who are Perfection, Beauty, Truth, Infinite and Essential Love, you are in me and around me. You fill me altogether . . . there is no particle of my body that you do not fill, and around me you are nearer than the air in which I move. How am I blessed! What happiness to be united so completely to Perfection itself; to live in it, to possess it living in myself! My God, you who are in me, in whom I am, let me know my happiness, and let me know my duty.

My God, give me a perpetual sense of your Presence, of your Presence in all around me, and at the same time that loving fear one feels in the presence of him one loves passionately, and which makes one, in the presence of one's Beloved, keep one's eyes upon him with great desire and firm purpose to do all that may please him and be for his good, and greatly fear to do or think anything that may displease or harm him.

In you, by you, and for you. Amen.

THE MIND OF GOD

I must try to know you, my God, so that I may love you better; the more I know you the more I shall love you, because in you all is perfect, lovable

MEDITATIONS OF A HERMIT

and admirable. To know you even a little better is to behold a more radiant, a more transparent beauty, to be transported out of myself by love. In you are all my thoughts, words and actions, my God. Your own Spirit is ever brooding. Your thoughts vary not. You contemplate yourself—your perfections and your works, present and future and through all the ages. You contemplate yourself, for you are Intellect. You love yourself, for you are Will—you love yourself infinitely of necessity, for you are Justice, and being Just, you love your own infinitely lovable and perfect Being. My God, you are in me, around me, my Saviour Jesus, my God, near me in the Host, and your thoughts are *Contemplation* and *Love*. You contemplate yourself, yourself alone, and in this contemplation of yourself are mirrored all your works. You have an infinite and sovereign love for yourself that must of necessity be, because it is the consequence that follows upon your infinite justice ; and in this love you love your own works ; on the one hand because they come from you and are the actions of an infinitely lovable Being, and on the other for their own beauty which is a fragment, and a reflection of the Divine Beauty which you have put into them, something good and lovable. And, again, you love them for their mere beauty, *quoniam bonus*, because you yourself are Good and it is of your nature to love.

THE WORDS AND ACTIONS OF GOD

You speak to men, my God, in two ways. Aloud, so to speak, and secretly. Aloud you speak by your inspired word, the Holy Scriptures, and secretly by your inspiring grace, by the inner voice by which you inspire your faithful. Do you speak only to the

RETREAT AT NAZARETH

Spirit? How and to whom do you speak? I know not, my God. You are infinite, I am a nothing, an atom. What can I know of you? Enough that I know you are the Infinite, the Essence, Perfection itself, and that is enough to shew me that I should love you without measure. I rejoice that I shall know you better in Heaven; and, seeing your Beauty, I shall love you more and more.

JESUS IN HIS INCARNATION AND BIRTH
November 6, 1897.

My God, all this happy day I shall meditate upon you. Yes, my God, you are constant and faithful. You still give me your Grace. Your Saints and Angels still are helping me, only I myself am helpless. You urge me on to good and load me with graces, and everything is helping me in Heaven and on earth, and I alone make obstacles through my cowardice and weakness and stupidity.

The Incarnation sprang from the goodness of God. The humility contained in this mystery is amazing, marvellous, astonishing. It shines with a dazzling brilliance. God, the Essence, the Infinite, Perfection, Creator, All-Powerful, the Great Sovereign Lord of All, becomes a man and takes on himself the body and soul of a man. He appears on earth as a man, and the humblest of men.

What is man's respect worth? Was it meant that God should seek to possess it? As he looks down upon the world from the height of his divinity all seem equal in his eyes, the great, the small, all like ants and worms to him. He disdained all false grandeur, which is in reality so very small, and had no wish to assume it himself. And as he came on earth to ransom us and teach us, he taught us from the very first, and all through his life, to despise human greatness and detach ourselves entirely from man's esteem. He was born, lived and died in deepest abjection, in the lowest humiliation, for he took once for all the lowest place so completely that no one has ever humbled himself lower than he did. It was to teach us that he put himself last so constantly, and to shew us that men and their respect are worth nothing ; that we must never despise those living in meanness and that the abject need never grieve for their humiliation. They are near to God, near to the King of Kings. He teaches us that since our conversation is not of this world we should make no matter of the forms of this world, but live only for that heavenly Kingdom which the God-man saw for ever here below by the Beatific Vision, and which we should see always with the eyes of Faith, walking in this world as though we were not of this world, without concern of outside things and busy with one thing only, with contemplating and loving our Heavenly Father and doing his Will.

RESOLUTIONS

In my thoughts, words and actions, whether directed to myself or my neighbour, I must never trouble about worldly position, celebrity, human esteem, but respect the poor equally with the rich. I must take as much trouble about the humblest workman as about a prince, since God appeared as a humble workman. Always, for myself, seek the lowest place, and be as low as my Master, so as to be with him and walk in his steps like a faithful servant and disciple (since in his infinite and incomprehensible goodness he lets me speak so), as a faithful brother, a faithful spouse. Thus I must arrange my life so

RETREAT AT NAZARETH

that I am the lowest and most despised of men, so that I live it beside my Master, my Lord, my Brother, my Spouse, my God who was the outcast of the people, and the reproach of the earth, a worm and no man.

It is my desire to live in poverty, abjection and suffering, in solitude and neglect, so that all my life I may be beside my Master, my Brother, my Spouse, my God, who lived thus all his life, and has given me the example ever since his birth.

THE HIDDEN LIFE OF JESUS

My Jesus, who art present near me, shew me what to think about your hidden life.

' He went down with them and went to Nazareth and was subject unto them.' He went down, lowered himself, humbled himself. It was a life of *humility*.

My God, you appear in the likeness of man, and becoming man you make yourself the lowest of men. Yours was a life of *abjection*. You took the lowest of the low places. You went down *with them*, to live their life, the life of the poor working people, living by their labour. Your life, like theirs, was poor, laborious, hard-working. They were humble and obscure. You lived in the shade of their obscurity. You went to Nazareth, a little village, lost, hidden in the mountains whence, it was said, ' no good came forth.' It was like a retreat. You were apart from the world and the towns, in this *retreat* you lived.

You were *subject* to them under their authority, as a son is to his father or his brother. It was a life of submission, of filial submission. You were a good obedient son. If your parents' wishes were

MEDITATIONS OF A HERMIT

not in perfect accord with your divine vocation you would not carry them out. You would 'rather obey God than man,' as when you stayed those three days in Jerusalem. But except in such a case when your vocation would claim you rather than the fulfilling of their wishes, you would fulfil them like the best of sons, not only obeying their smallest wish, but forestalling them, doing all that could give them pleasure, consoling them, making life sweet and pleasant for them, trying, with all your heart, to make them happy, being a model for all sons, having great thought for your parents, that is to say, in the measure allowed you by your vocation. But your vocation was to be perfect, and you *could* only be perfect, O Eternal Son of God. Thus during those thirty years you were, as a Son, always tender, considerate, sympathetic, kind. You gave all the happiness you could to your parents, helping, supporting, encouraging them in their daily labour, taking the greater part on yourself to save them fatigue, never crossing them except when the Son of God required it, and then what sweetness and gentleness you would shew, so that your non-acquiescence would be sweeter to them than obedience; it would be like a heavenly dew, full of that grace and delicacy and consideration with which a beautiful soul makes life sweet to others. Nothing was left out that could make your parents' life happy and make their little home a heaven.

This was your life at Nazareth, and it is my infinite happiness and incomparable grace to live in this beloved Nazareth.

Yours was the life of a model Son with your humble working parents. It made up half of your life, that half that was of the earth though it spread a heavenly perfume through Heaven. This was the

RETREAT AT NAZARETH

visible half. The other invisible half was your life in God which was perpetual contemplation. You worked and helped your parents and had holy tender intercourse with them and prayed with them during the day, but in the solitude and shadow of the night your soul poured itself out in silence!

Always, continually, you prayed, for praying is to be with God, and you are God. But your human soul continued this contemplation through the night as, all through the day, it was united to your divinity. Your life was a constant outpouring before God, your soul looked always upon God, always contemplating him. What then was this prayer that was the half of your life at Nazareth? Before and above all things, it was adoration, contemplation, silent adoration which is the most eloquent of all praise. *Tibi silentium laus.* A silent worship expressing the most passionate declaration of love, for the love of worship is the most radiant love of all loves.

Then, secondarily, taking up less time, less prolonged, *thanksgiving*, first for the glory of God, that God is God. Then for grace given on earth to all creatures. Then the cry for *pardon*, pardon for all sins against God, pardon for those who do not ask pardon, acts of contrition for the whole world, sorrow that God is offended. Then *supplication*; supplicating for God's Glory, that God may be glorified by all his creatures, that his reign may come amongst them, that his Will may be done in them as it is in the Angels and that these poor creatures may receive all they need spiritually and temporally, and may be delivered from evil in this world and the next. And that the Grace of God may abound in all those who by his will have drawn close to Our Lord, upon father, mother, relations and friends, and all who love him and have given themselves to him.

THE PUBLIC LIFE OF JESUS

My Lord Jesus, it will be sweet to pass another day with you. All my days should so be spent: working, praying, talking. Always, except when I sleep, I should pray and think of you. I do it so badly, but I so much long to do it better that I hope to attain it by your grace. Give me this grace. But to-day I must not only do this, but I must do nothing else; not only must I contemplate you, but I must look at nothing else but you. What happiness to contemplate you and how good you are to give me this joy. How blessed I am.

My God, here am I at your feet in my cell, all around is in silence, all sleeps. I am perhaps the only soul in Nazareth, at this moment, at your feet. What have I done to merit this grace? Thank you, thank you. I am grateful. I adore you from the depths of my soul. I am yours and only yours. All my being is yours: it is of necessity without any will of mine, but also it is so voluntary, with all my heart's will. Do with me what you will. Let me make this retreat as you wish. 'Be you perfect as your Father in Heaven is perfect,' you answer. Ah! then, my God, let this, my retreat, be perfect, in you, for you, through you. Amen.

What then, my Lord Jesus, was your public life?

'I tried to save men by word and by works of mercy. Before, in my life at Nazareth, I was content to save them by prayer and penance. Now I shew my zeal for souls publicly. But though my life became more active it was always partly solitary and was always a life of prayer and penance and interior

RETREAT AT NAZARETH

recollection. Often I went into the solitude apart, at night or for days together, to pray alone. Except for the time devoted to preaching the Gospel, mine was a life of solitude. It was a life of fatigue, long journeys, long sermons, and days in the desert without shelter or shade cannot be without fatigue and physical suffering, intemperate weather, nights without shelter, uncertain nourishment snatched when work permitted ; all these mean suffering. Then there was *moral* suffering : men's ingratitude, their deaf ears, their ill will, their hard hearts, my healing hand laid daily on all sorts of sufferings of the human body. Souls saved, so many lost to be found, such human suffering, that of the righteous, that of my Mother, the vision ever growing nearer and greater of my Passion ; of enmities as the only response to my words of salvation, to my words of love offered to all men ; above all, the ingratitude of that "faithless and perverse generation" wounding my tender compassionate Heart.

PERSECUTION

'I was persecuted everywhere and by all men ; at Jerusalem and at Nazareth. I was stoned and cast out, everywhere, in towns, and villages. Pharisees, Scribes, Sadducees and Herodians, all sought my death ; they set traps for me, insulted me secretly and publicly, called me possessed, devil, seducer, impostor, and denounced me to the priests. The Gentiles despised me as an Israelite. Everywhere my life was in danger either from Herod or from the Pharisees. I was forced to flee from place to place. Often they laid hands on me, and by a miracle I was saved. I had to shew courage before men. I reproached them openly for their faults.

MEDITATIONS OF A HERMIT

I even punished them and shewed up the hypocrites publicly, and proclaimed divine Truth against its most burning contradictions. I proclaimed the truth before a turbulent crowd of dissenters. I worked miracles and did acts in the Temple and in the synagogues, in which I was accused and condemned. I preached courageously in the Temple at Jerusalem to people who always had stones in their hands to throw at me, and in the synagogues of Galilee where the Pharisees ground their teeth and wove a thousand plots to trap me.

'*Love for the Truth* I ever had, for I am the Truth, but in preaching it and spreading it zealously amidst perils and sufferings I shewed forth its value.

Humility. ' I shewed humility when I let John baptize me. I humbled myself when I so often forbade my apostles to proclaim that I was the Son of God. I humbled myself when I hid my good deeds and miracles, saying to those I healed, " Tell no man." I humbled myself fleeing from town to town in times of persecution. I, the all powerful, who could with justice destroy my enemies by a word.'

THE PASSION OF JESUS

Now, my God, I will meditate on your Passion ; inspire my thought yourself, for by myself I am incapable of vision. The Passion . . . What a memory ! The blows and stripes given by the servants of the high priest. ' Prophesy who it was that struck you.' The silence before Herod and Pilate. The scourging ; the crowning with

RETREAT AT NAZARETH

thorns ; the way of the cross ; the crucifixion ; the cross.
' Father, into thy hands I commend my spirit.' My God, what pictures these words bring to my mind. *What tears to shed* if I love you. *What remorse* when I think that it was to expiate my sins that you suffered there. *What emotion* when I think that as you underwent all these torments of your own free will it was to shew your love down through all the centuries. *Remorse* that I love you so little. Remorse that I do so little *penance* for the sins for which you did so great a penance. What longing to love you in return and to prove to you my love by all possible means. ' He that loves me loves my commandments.' There is no greater love than to give one's life for the beloved.' To do your commandments. ' Mandata.' That is to say, carry out not only the orders but the counsels and to conform to the merest precept and follow the least example. One of the greatest of your precepts is to imitate you. ' Follow me. He that follows me does not walk in darkness. I have given you the example so that what I have done you should do. The servant is perfect if he is like his master.' I must follow as minutely as possible all your teaching, all your example in this life, and die for your name. This is how I can prove that I love you and learn to love you more. You tell me so in the Gospels, my God. Now love asks still one more thing, my God, and the Gospel shews that too. Not by words of yours but by the Blessed Virgin and Mary Magdalen at the foot of the cross. *Stabat Mater.*

Compassion to weep for your sorrows. Truly this would be a great grace. Of myself I am incapable of drawing tears from this heart of stone at the thought of your cross, so horribly hard is it.

MEDITATIONS OF A HERMIT

But I ask from you the gift of compassion, for since I owe it to you I ought to ask it, so that I may give it to you. I ought to ask from you all that I am bound to give you.

Since, my God, from the depths of your mercy, from the treasure of your mysterious and infinite goodness you have granted me the grace to live under the sky and in this land where you lived, to tread the soil that you trod, that you watered with your tears, with the sweat of your brow, and with your Precious Blood, let me not dwell in these places that are witnesses of your sorrows with a hardened heart. Let me kiss with tears the traces of your feet passing to Gethsemani, along the Way of the Cross to the pretorium and to Calvary. Turn my stony heart to a compassionate one and give me grace to kiss your footprints with the tears you would have me shed from my soul and from my heart. O my Lord, my King, my Master, my Spouse, my Brother, my Beloved, my Saviour, my God.

Resolution. Ask, desire, and if it is God's will to suffer martyrdom, that I may shew a full measure of love for Jesus. Have zeal for Souls, a burning love for Souls which have all been bought at the same price. Despise no one but desire the greatest good for every man, for all are covered, as with a mantle, by the precious blood of Jesus. Do all I can for the salvation of all souls, according to my circumstances, since they have cost Jesus so dear and were and still are so much beloved by him. He, perfect, holy ; I for whom Jesus had so much consideration that he gave all his Precious Blood for me. *Have a great desire for perfection and believe all to be possible for the Glory of God* when my confessor directs me to do something. How can God refuse

RETREAT AT NAZARETH

his grace after he has given me his Precious Blood ? Have *an infinite horror of sin and of imperfection which leads to it*, since it cost Jesus so dear. *Sorrow for the sins of others because they offend God*, since he holds sin in such horror that he had to expiate it by such suffering. *Absolute confidence and unshaken faith in the love of God* proved by his suffering. *Humility* in the thought of all he has done for me, and how little I have done for him. *Desire for suffering* to return him love for love, to imitate him, and not to wear a crown of roses when his is made of thorns, to expiate my sins that he has so painfully expiated, to enter into his work, offer myself with him, though I am nothing, as a sacrifice, a victim, for the sanctification of all men.

JESUS IN HIS RESURRECTION AND HIS ASCENSION

You rose again and ascended into Heaven. Now are you glorified. You suffer no more and never more will suffer. You are happy and will be happy for ever more. My God, if I love you how happy I should be. If I desire your good above everything how I should rejoice, what satisfaction I should feel. My God, you are blessed for all eternity. You lack nothing now. You are for ever and infinitely happy. I, too, am happy, for I love you above all things. To me, too, nothing is lacking. I am as though in Heaven; happen what may I am blessed through your blessedness.

Resolution. When we are depressed, discouraged about ourselves, others and everything, let us think of Jesus in glory, sitting at the right hand of the Father, for ever happy. If we love him as we ought, the happiness of the Infinite Being should take away all sadness that arises from our finite natures, and looking upon the happiness of our God, our souls should be jubilant and the sadness that weighs us down should vanish like the clouds before the sunshine. For God is happy. Rejoice then without end, for all the ills of created things are but an atom beside the joy of the Creator. There always will be sorrow in our lives, and it is right there should be because of the love we bear to ourselves and to all men, and also because of the love we bear to Jesus, and the remembrance of his sufferings; because of the desire we should feel for justice, that is to say, for the glory of God, and the pain we should feel when we see God unjustly insulted. But these sorrows, though they are justified, should not dwell in our hearts, they should be but passing; the feeling which should remain, and should be our normal state of mind, to which we should return always, is joy for the glory of God, the joy that Jesus now no longer suffers and will never suffer more, that he is happy for ever, at the right hand of God.

JESUS IN THE HOLY EUCHARIST

You dwell, my Lord Jesus, in the Holy Eucharist. You are here, within a few feet of me, in the Tabernacle. Your body, your soul, your humanity, your divinity, your whole being is here in its twofold nature. How close you are, my God, my Saviour, my Jesus, my Brother, my Spouse, my Beloved. You were no nearer to the Blessed Virgin and S. Joseph in the cave at Bethlehem, in the house at Nazareth, than you are to me here now, so often, in the Tabernacle. S. Mary Magdalen was no nearer to you when she sat at your feet at Bethany

RETREAT AT NAZARETH

than I am at the foot of the altar. You were no nearer your apostles when you were seated in their midst than you are to me now, my God. How happy, oh ! how happy I am. It is sweet to converse with you alone in my cell in the silence of the night and you are present as God as well as by your Grace ; but, still, if I were to stay in my cell when I might be before the Blessed Sacrament is as though, when you were at Bethany, Mary Magdalen had left you alone to go and think about you in her chamber. It is a good and pious act to kiss the places you have sanctified in your mortal life, the stones of Gethsemani and of Calvary, the soil of the Way of the Cross, the waves of the sea at Galilee, but to prefer that to your Tabernacle would be to leave the living Jesus at my side, him alone, and to go off alone to venerate dead stones where he is no longer. It would be like leaving the room in which is his divine companionship, to go and kiss the floor of a room where he once was, but is no more. To leave the Tabernacle to go and venerate statues is to leave Jesus living at my side to go into another and salute his image.

When one loves one feels that all hours spent beside the Beloved are well spent. One's time is best spent so, except when we are called elsewhere to work for the Beloved.

Wherever the Sacred Host is there is the living God. There is your Saviour as truly as when he lived and spoke in Judea, and Galilee, and as truly as he is now in Paradise. Never miss a communion through your own fault ; communion is more than life, more than all the wealth of the world, more than the whole universe : it is me, Jesus. How can you prefer something else to me. How can you, even if you love me a little, of your own will forego the

MEDITATIONS OF A HERMIT

grace I offer you of entering within you. Love me with an open and a simple heart.

JESUS IN HIS LIFE IN THE CHURCH AND THE SOULS OF THE FAITHFUL

My Lord Jesus, you are ' with us even to the end of the world.' Not only in the Holy Eucharist, but also in your grace. Your grace dwells in the Church, it dwells also in every faithful soul. The Church is your spouse, and so also is the faithful soul your spouse. Your grace works in them, conforming them to yourself. It works without ceasing in the Church to perfect her. She grows more perfect by the increasing number of her saints. Always new ones are being added to the old ones, and the crown of saints is completed every day by new jewels; she grows more perfect through her dogmas being more and more clearly defined, and her liturgy being more and more completely organized, by her discipline; she grows more perfect through the fresh crosses which you lay upon her daily and the victories she wins daily against the Prince of this world. She grows more perfect by the persecutions that she bears in one century after another, and in her suffering she grows more and more like to her Spouse; she grows more perfect through the merits of her members added daily to the merit of past days. A sum of holiness growing unceasingly, a sum which glorifies God anew, adding itself always to the ancient glory which is ever living before the Lord. She grows more perfect by the multitude of masses, by the tabernacles, by the communions in which Jesus is daily offered on earth to God, fresh offerings adding themselves to former ones; she grows

RETREAT AT NAZARETH

more perfect because the grace of to-day added to the past graces cannot fail to carry the spouse from height to height ever nearer to her Lover. Jesus is the soul of the Church, he gives to her what the soul gives to the body—*life*. He gives her immortal life so that she shall never be destroyed, he gives her *light*, making her infallible in declaring the truth ; he works through her and carries on through her the work that he began whilst he lived amongst men. He works for the glory of God through the sanctifying of man. This work is the aim of the Church as it was the aim of Christ ; through her Jesus accomplishes it unceasingly through the centuries.

You dwell in the souls of the faithful, Lord. ' We enter in to her and there we make our dwelling.' You become, as it were, the soul of their soul, your grace supports it in everything, enlightens its intellect, directs its will ; it is no longer the soul that acts, it is you who work in her. You give her life, the life of grace, sowing the seeds of the glorified life with increasing abundance ; you give her the truth and you establish it in her, you make her understand it, you unbind her eyes and make her see all things with the eyes of faith ; you set her thus in the divine life high above the shadows of the world. You continue your work in her. The end of all men, as it is the end of the earth, and your own aim, my Lord Jesus, is the glory of God, that is to say, the outward manifestation of his glory, and the sanctification of men. You love us : therefore the more perfect we are the greater is your consolation ; we should desire with all our might to please you, for you tell us to love you with all our strength. It is our duty to desire to be as perfect as possible . . . make then our thoughts, words, actions, like

MEDITATIONS OF A HERMIT

to yours, live in us, reign in us that it may no longer be we that live, but you, my God, that live in us, and who, using our bodies and our souls, which we give to you without reserve, may continue through them your life and your work in this world. That work is the glory of God and the salvation of men in that measure which you have decreed yourself in your eternal designs ; in you, by you, and for you. Amen. Amen. Amen.

MYSELF AND MY PAST LIFE
THE MERCY OF GOD[1]

My Lord Jesus, inspire my thoughts, inspire my words. If, in my former meditations, I was powerless, alone, how much more am I now. It is not the matter that is lacking ; on the contrary, it is crushing. What mercy you have shewn me. Mercy in the past, in the present, at every minute of my life, before my birth and before all time. I am drowned, flooded in them, they envelop and protect me on all sides. Oh, my God, we are all bound to sing of your mercies who have all been created for Glory and bought by the blood of Jesus, by your blood, my Jesus, you, here by my side in this Tabernacle. But if it is the duty of all, how much more is it my duty to do so, I who, since my birth, have been surrounded with so many graces. I was the son of a saintly mother, from whom I learnt to know you and love you and to pray to you as soon as I could understand a few words. My first recollection is the prayer she made me say every morning and evening. ' God bless my father,

---

[1] This meditation, which is, I think, the only fragment in this volume that has been published before, has already been given in the *Biography of Charles de Foucauld*. But as it forms part of the Retreat at Nazareth it seems best to reproduce it here.

RETREAT AT NAZARETH

mother, grandfather, and grandmother and my little sister.' I remember my education, my first Communion. I was well prepared, surrounded by my Christian family ; it was a day full of sweetness, I found encouragement and perseverance in the example of those I loved around me, and you, my God, rooted in my soul such love for them, my parents and my family, that all the storms that followed could never tear my affections from them. So that you were able to use this affection later on to save me from death, drowned in sin as I was. For when, in spite of all these graces, I had begun to separate myself from you, you could call me back by the voice of those I loved, my affection for them alone prevented me from falling into the extremes of sin. Even so, alas ! I strayed further and further away from you, my Lord and my Life, and my life was more like a death in your eyes. But still you kept the remembrance of the past in my heart like a fire under the ashes, with a respect for good, and an attachment to certain good and lovely souls, a regard for the Catholic Church and for her priests. Though all my faith had vanished this respect and esteem remained intact. Other graces you gave me, my God, the love of study, of reading, of beauty, hatred of vice and ugliness. I sinned, but neither approved of nor loved sin. You made me feel in it such emptiness and sadness as I have never felt at any other time. It came upon me when I found myself alone in my room at night, it made me dumb and miserable in the midst of what men call festivities. I was the moving spirit in these, but in the midst of them I felt dumb, disgusted, infinitely bored. You gave me that vague disquietude of a bad conscience which though it may be asleep is not yet dead. At no other time have

MEDITATIONS OF A HERMIT

I felt such sadness, depression and unrest. So, my God, it was a gift from you. I was very far from realizing it. How good you were. And whilst you kept my soul from death you preserved my body from harm, for if I had died then I should have been in Hell. I escaped marvellously from riding accidents, duels were averted, dangerous expeditions were carried through without disaster, you brought me miraculously through perilous journeys, you gave me health in poisonous climates and in great fatigues. O my God, your hand was leading me and I felt it so little. How good you are. How you have kept and guarded me. You sheltered me under your wings when I did not even believe in your existence. And keeping me thus safe, time passed, and you saw the moment had come for me to return to the fold. You untied in spite of myself all the evil knots that held me from you, and loosened even those good ties that might have kept me from returning to the beloved family, in which it was your will I should find my salvation, and which might have prevented my being one day altogether yours. At the same time you made me study deeply, living a hidden life, a life of poverty and solitude. My heart was alienated from you, but I was living in a cleaner atmosphere. It was as yet neither light nor truth, but it was not such deep mire, nor such hateful evil. Gradually the ground was cleared, the waters of the deluge still covered the earth, but slowly they were sinking and the rain had ceased. You had broken down the barriers, softened my heart, prepared the ground, burnt up the thorns and the weeds. By force of circumstances I led a chaste life, and presently, by the winter of 1866, when I returned to my family in Paris, chastity had become to me a pleasure,

RETREAT AT NAZARETH

a necessity. It is you who did this for me, my Lord, you only, and I had no part in it. How good you have been ! You have saved me from so many guilty backslidings. You have preserved me most mercifully. Your hand alone has saved me from the beginning to the end. How good you are ! My soul had to be prepared for truth. The devil is too much the master of a soul that knows not chastity, for truth to find an entrance. You could not enter, my God, into a soul in which impure passions were reigning. But because you wished to enter into my soul, oh, my Good Shepherd, you drove your enemy out yourself. Then having driven him out by force, seeing me so weak and helpless to keep my own soul pure you gave me a good guardian, so strong and gentle that he left no chance of entry to the devil, because he gave me pleasure and delight in the beauty of chastity. My God, how shall I sing your mercies ! When you had emptied my soul of its filth, and confided it to your Angels, then you began to take possession of it yourself, for though it had received all these graces, as yet it did not know you. You were working in it, transforming with power and swiftness, and still it remained completely ignorant of you. Then you inspired me with a love of virtue, of pagan virtues. I searched for them in the writings of the pagan philosophers, and I found nothing but emptiness and weariness. Then by chance my eyes fell upon some pages of a Christian writer, and you made me feel their warmth and beauty.[1]

You gave me then the idea that in such writings I might find, if not the truth (for I did not believe it possible for men to know the truth), at least some teaching about virtue, and you inspired me to seek

[1] This was probably Bossuet's *Élévations sur les Mystères*.

MEDITATIONS OF A HERMIT

in Christian writings for teaching about pagan virtues. Thus I grew to know the mysteries of religion. At the same time you drew me closer and closer to those beautiful souls that I found again in my family, whom I had so passionately loved in childhood and youth. I found again my youthful admiration of these souls and you inspired them, too, to receive me as a Prodigal Son who should never be allowed to feel that he had left his home. They were as good to me as though I had never failed them. I grew more and more intimate with this beloved family, and in their atmosphere of goodness I lived again. It was like spring reviving the wintry earth. In their sweet sunshine grew up so great a need for good and hatred of evil that it became impossible to me to fall back into certain sins. I cherished my pure life, sin was driven out of my heart, my Good Angel had taken possession of it and to him you added an earthly Angel. Thus, at the beginning of 1886, after six months of happy family life, I loved and revered goodness, but still I did not know you. . . . O God of goodness, what ingenious means, by what devious ways, by what sweet persuasions did you make yourself known to me. Such a chain of strange circumstances drew me to you. Solitude, anxieties in the sickness of the loved ones, searchings, longings, my return to Paris after strange events. Such inspiration of grace in my need of solitude and recollection and reading. I, who had not faith in you, began to haunt the churches, my soul was troubled, my search for virtue became an anguish and I prayed, ' My God ! if you exist, let me know you.' All this was your work, my God, and yours alone. A great soul was helping in the work, silently, gently, in perfect goodness, but though its

RETREAT AT NAZARETH

sweet atmosphere made itself felt by me, it remained passive. You, my Jesus, my Saviour, were working within and without. By the beauty of this soul in which goodness seemed to me so lovable I was drawn to love 'virtue. My heart was taken captive by it. You drew me to love truth by the beauty of this soul, and then you granted me four graces. The first was the inspiration of this thought !—this soul is so intelligent that the religion in which it believes so deeply cannot be so mad as I think it ; the second inspired the thought that if the Christian religion is not madness, perhaps the Truth which I can find in nothing else on earth, nor in any philosophy, is to be found there ; the third grace told me to study this religion and to find a teacher to instruct me in the Catholic Faith, and the fourth led me to seek the Abbé Huvelin as that teacher.[1] When you made me enter his confessional, one day at the end of October (between the 27th and the 30th I think it was), you gave me the best of all, my God. If there is joy in Heaven for one sinner that repents there must have been joy the day that I went into the confessional. Since that day my life has been one long series of blessings. You put me under the wings of that Saint and there I stayed. You have borne me along by his hands and I have received one grace after another. I asked him for instruction in religion, and he made me kneel down and make my confession and sent me straightway to Communion. I cannot help weeping when I think of it, and would not if I could, for it is right that I should still weep tears of gratitude at the remembrance of such mercies. How good you have been. What have I done to

---

[1] The Abbé Huvelin, a priest, once a pupil of the *Ecole Normal Superieure*. He is remembered in Paris as a very holy man.

MEDITATIONS OF A HERMIT

receive such happiness, for, ever since, my God, I have known a series of blessings, a rising tide of graces. Direction (and what direction !), prayer, reading, the help of daily Mass, a habit established on the first day of my new life ; frequent communion, frequent confession after a few weeks ; direction that became more and more intimate and frequent, embracing my whole life, which became a life of obedience in the smallest things, and obedience to what a master ! Communion became almost daily, the desire for the religious life was born and grew in me and was confirmed, and then quite apart from my own will events occurred which forced me to detach myself from material things that had such charm for me and which would have held back my soul and kept me tied to the world. These ties you broke violently like so many others. How good you are, my God, to have so broken up and destroyed all around me that might have kept me from belonging to you alone. You gave me a profound sense of the vanity and falseness of the world, the vast gulf that lies between the perfect life of the Gospel, and that which one leads in the world. You gave me a tender and a growing love for you, my Lord Jesus, a love of prayer, of faith in your words, a deep sense of the duty of almsgiving and a great desire to imitate you. Those words of the Abbé Huvelin, spoken in a sermon, were ineffaceably deeply engraved on my soul. 'You took always the lowest place and did it so completely that no one ever since has been able to wrest it from you,' and I trusted to make you the greatest sacrifice I was able to offer you, that of leaving for ever my family in which was laid up all my happiness and going afar off to live and die. I sought a life in conformity

RETREAT AT NAZARETH

with yours, where I might share your abjection and poverty, your humble labour, your buried life, your obscurity, and I found it clearly pointed out to me in a last retreat at Clamart. On January 15, 1890, the sacrifice was made through grace given to me at your hands. There followed *La Trappe*, daily Communion, all that I learnt in my seven years of religious life, the blessings of *Notre Dame des Neiges*, the theology and philosophy I studied in my reading, the development of my own doubted vocation to a life of abjection and obscurity. After three and a half years of waiting, the Vicar-General told me on January 23, 1897, that it was the will of God that I should follow this attraction which urged me to pursue the life of abjection and humble labour in deep obscurity, the vision of which had been with me for so long. I left for the Holy Land as a pilgrim and I arrived at Nazareth, and the first Wednesday I was there you let me, through the intercession of S. Joseph, enter as servant at the Convent of S. Clare. I was filled with peace and happiness, and felt deep consoling grace and marvellous happiness.

MISERICORDIAS DOMINI IN AETERNUM CANTABO . . . VENITE ET VIDETE, QUONIAM SUAVIS EST DOMINUS

I faint, my God, before such mercies ; I implore the Blessed Virgin and the Saints and all Holy Souls to thank for me, for I faint under these Graces. Oh, my Spouse, how much have you done for me. What do you ask of me whom you have thus so loaded. What do you expect from me. My God, be you yourself, my thanks, my gratitude, my faith, my love, I faint, I fail, inspire my thoughts, my

MEDITATIONS OF A HERMIT

words, my works, that all may express my gratitude, and that you may be glorified in me. Amen. Amen. Amen.

MY FUTURE ON EARTH, MY DEATH, JUDGEMENT, HEAVEN OR HELL

Pardon and *Misericordias Domini in aeternum Cantabo*. Such are my past and my present. What is to be my future? Is it to be long or short on earth? Happy or sorrowful? Holy as I long for it to be, or full of sin? from which I implore you to save me. No one can know. It will be as you will it, my God. I only ask that it may not be spent in offending you. That cannot be your will. You have commanded us all to be perfect, and you have loaded me with graces and said, ' To him that hath much more shall be given.' So whatever may be my future, whether long or a day's span, happy or sorrowful, it must be your will that it be sanctified. What shall I do that it may be so?

' Follow me and only me. Do not come to Bethany to see me and also Lazarus. Come to see me and only me. Ask me what I did, study the Scriptures, study also the Saints, not so as to follow them, themselves, but to see how they followed me, and to take from each of them what you think comes from me, is inspired by me, is done in imitation of me, and follow me, me alone. Imagine yourself as in the house at Nazareth. You have given yourself to me. I will lead you for my greater glory, for the great consolation of my Heart, since that is what you desire and ask for.'

Yes, yes, my Lord and my God, I desire and ask for only that. Let it be so in you, by you, and for you. Amen. Amen.

RETREAT AT NAZARETH

'This life will be followed by death. You wish for a Martyr's death. You know how cowardly you are, but you know too that you can do all things in him who gives strength, that I am All Powerful in my creatures. Ask night and day for it, but always with this condition, that it be my will, and for my glory and my pleasure which I know you desire and pray for above all things. And have confidence ; I will grant what you ask, that which is for my greater glory. It is good to ask for this, for "there is no greater love than to give your life for the beloved," and it is right to wish to give me this " greatest love of all." '

'What will eternity and judgement be for you? As your life has been so will they be. If you have denied yourself, if you have carried your cross and have followed me, if, remembering the graces and wonderful mercies that I have shewn, you have born fruit to those talents which I have given you ; if you are faithful to your vocation, obedient to your director, grateful, faithful, loving and gentle, you will be happy in your judgement and blessed in your eternity. But if you give way to your cowardice and sensuality and sloth, to timidity and self-seeking, falsehood and all other bad passions that the devil will at once seek to arouse in you again ; if you relax your watch for a moment, and if my fatherly hand does not hold you up, your judgement and your eternity will be the more terrible for having misused so many graces. It would indeed be horrible if the prodigal son were to revolt against his father and offend him after having been taken back by him. Your conduct would be a thousand times worse since for the last eleven years you have received almost every day my body and my soul, my humanity and my divinity to nourish you. " Therefore watch and pray, for the spirit is willing, but the flesh is weak." '

MYSELF, MY PRESENT LIFE
THE VIRTUE OF FAITH

In all things let God be your object. God is our Creator, we belong to him, we must bear fruit for him as the tree does for its master ; God is infinitely lovable, we should love him to the full capacity of our souls, therefore we must contemplate him always, keep him always in our mind, that all we do may be for him, just as when one loves one does everything in the thought of one's Beloved. Everything comes to us from God ; our being, our preservation, our body and spirit. Since we have received everything from God, it is right that we should give back all things to him. ' Render unto Cæsar the things that are Cæsar's, and to God the things that are God's.' Our whole being, our whole existence, our every heart's beat belongs to God, for all comes from him and through him.

You could not have faith, O Lord Jesus, because you had perfect vision, but you enjoined it upon us unceasingly. Faith is that which makes us believe from the depths of our souls all the dogmas of our religion, all the truths that our religion teaches us, all that the Gospel holds and all that the Church sets before us. The just man lives truly by this Faith, for it replaces for him the greater part of his natural senses ; it so transforms all things that the senses are of little use to the soul, which through them is only deceived, whilst Faith shews it realities. Where the eye sees but a poor man, the Faith sees Jesus. Where the ear hears curses and persecution, the Faith sings : ' Rejoice and be joyful.' The

RETREAT AT NAZARETH

touch feels only blows and stonings, but Faith says ' be glad that you are deemed worthy to suffer for the name of Christ.' Our taste perceives only a wafer of unleavened bread, Faith shews us our Saviour Jesus, God and Man, Soul and Body. The smell perceives only incense, Faith tells us that the true incense is ' the fasting of the Saints.' The senses lead us astray to created beauty, Faith thinks of the eternal beauty and despises all created things, for they are as nothing and as dust beside that beauty. The senses hold pain in horror, Faith blesses it as a marriage crown that unites it to its Beloved. The senses rebel against injuries, but Faith blesses them. ' Bless those that curse you ' ; to Faith they seem merited because she thinks of her sins, she finds them sweet, for in them she shares the lot of Jesus. The senses are full of curiosity, Faith is content to know nothing, she thirsts to bury herself, and longs to pass her life motionless before the Tabernacle. The senses love riches and honour ; Faith holds them in horror. All greatness is an abomination before God. ' Blessed are the poor.' She adores the poverty and lowliness with which Jesus covered his life as though with a garment that he never cast off. The senses hold suffering in horror, Faith blesses it as a gift from the hand of Jesus, a bit of his cross which he lets us carry. The senses take fright at that which they call danger, at all that might mean pain or death ; but Faith is afraid of nothing ; she knows nothing can happen to her but what is the will of God. ' I have counted every hair of your head,' and whatever God wishes will always be for her good. ' All that happens is for the good of my elect.' Thus in everything that may happen, sorrow or joy, health or sickness, life or death, she is content and fears

MEDITATIONS OF A HERMIT

nothing. The senses are anxious about the future and ask how we shall live to-morrow, but Faith feels no anxiety. 'Be not anxious,' says Jesus, 'consider the lilies of the field, see how I nourish and clothe the birds, you are of more value than they. Seek you first the Kingdom of God and all things shall be added to you.' The senses cling to the family and to possessions; Faith hastens to leave both. ' He who leaves, for my sake, father or mother, house and land, shall receive a hundredfold in this world and in the other life eternal.'

Thus Faith illumines all with a new light, different to the life of the senses, more brilliant, of another kind. He who lives by Faith has his soul full of new thoughts, new tastes, new impressions; new horizons open before him, marvellous horizons lit with a new light, and with a divine beauty surrounded with new truths of which the world is not aware. Thus he who believes begins a new life opposed to that of the world, to whom his acts seem like madness. The world is in the darkness of night, the man of faith is in full light.

HOPE

Speak to me, my God, of Hope! How can thoughts of Hope have their origin in this wretched world. Do they not spring from Heaven? All we see, all we feel, all we are shew us our nothingness. How could we know, unless you had told us, that we were created to be brothers and co-heirs with Jesus? Mother of Love and holy Hope, pray to your Son Jesus for me and inspire my thoughts. I would see the vision that Hope shews me, of being one day in Heaven, in company with the Blessed Virgin and the Saints, seeing you, loving you,

RETREAT AT NAZARETH

possessing you for all eternity. My God and my all. A Vision of peace, of heavenly peace. You grant us this vision of Hope. You ever enjoin it upon us. It carries us far above ourselves, above our very dreams. The symbol of Hope is an anchor, and so it is in reality a strong, firm anchor. However great may be my sins it is my duty to hope. You forbid me to despair. However ungrateful and tepid and cowardly I may be, however much I may abuse your graces, my God, you forbid me to be discouraged at the sight of my misery and to say to myself, ' I can go no further, the road to Heaven is too steep, I must go back and roll like a stone to the bottom of the hill.' You forbid me to say when I see myself renew my faults every day (I ask pardon for them every day, and every day I fall into them again), ' I shall never correct myself; holiness is not for me. What have I in common with Heaven ? I am not worthy to enter.' You forbid me to say when I look at the infinite graces with which you have loaded me and at the baseness of my own present life, that I have misused these graces too often ; that I ought to be a Saint and I am a sinner ; that I cannot cure myself : it is too difficult. That I am nothing but pride and misery. That after all that God has done for me there is no good in me and I shall never get to Heaven.

You bid me hope always, in spite of all, that I shall get enough grace to change my life and attain to glory. What is there in common between Heaven and me, my misery and its perfections ? There is your Divine Heart, my Lord Jesus, to link these two things so unlike one another. The love of the Father, who so loved the world that he gave his only Son. I am bound always to hope because you command it, and always to believe in your love and in your power, since you have promised me so much. Yes, when I think of all you have done for me I feel I should have such confidence in your mercy that however ungrateful and unworthy I may feel myself I shall always hope in it and count upon it. I may be certain that you will always be ready to receive me like the father of the Prodigal Son ; that you will never cease to call me and give me the grace to come to your feet.

COURAGE

My Lord Jesus, speak to me about courage. Give me courage, for perhaps I lack it more than anything else, though so many things are lacking in me. This morning, again, I three times was wanting in courage. Twice I woke without rising, and at the ringing of the Angelus I hesitated to go out because of the rain. Pardon me, pardon me ! As though it was not a grace blessed a thousand times to awake early so as to be early in converse with you, to be the earlier at your feet, at your knees, my head between your hands, telling you that I love you. As though to wake were not to be called by you, as though when I awake there are not shining before my eyes the words ' It is the hour to love God.'

'You need courage before men against their threats and against their seductions, against the persecutions of the world as against its sweetness, against the wicked in company with the Saints. Courage to bear unkindness and not to be weakened by kindness, to be with all and in all that which I wish you to be so that you may bear mockery, contradiction, blows, wounds and death as my faithful soldier. Also to resist affection, tenderness,

RETREAT AT NAZARETH

love, soft words, praise and delicate gifts, that you may neither fear to hurt yourself nor any other, but only me. You need courage to fight against the devil, against terrors and troubles, temptations, attractions, darkness and false lights, against fears, depression, dissipations, phantoms, false shame and, above all, fear (for this is the weapon he always wields, especially with you, who are so timid and unfaithful), through all of which means he will seek to tear you from me.'

HUMILITY

You said, O my God, 'Learn of me, for I am meek and humble of heart,' and you gave us a true example of humility. You, God, made yourself man, you made yourself the lowest of men, a humble workman in that little Nazareth where I have lived, and when you passed from the hidden life to your public life what humility you shewed in your words and acts, in your teaching and your example. When you work miracles you command that nothing should be said of them, that no one should be told when you let your apostles see your glory, you tell them to be silent until your Resurrection. When you are called to a sick man you go at once. When anyone asks you for something you do it at once. When you are persecuted you flee. In nothing do you shew yourself to be God, King, All Powerful. When you are roughly spoken to you answer gently. When you are driven out you depart without speaking. When you are refused hospitality you go elsewhere. Everywhere you humble yourself, and in your teaching it is the same. 'Woe to the rich, it is more difficult for them to enter into Heaven than for a camel to pass

MEDITATIONS OF A HERMIT

through the eye of a needle.' 'The Son of Man is meek and humble of heart.' 'Unless you become like little children you shall not enter the Kingdom of Heaven.' 'He who exalts himself shall be humbled, and he that humbles himself shall be exalted.' All pride is an abomination before God. Do not let yourselves be called Master. Take the lowest place. He shall be the greatest amongst you who makes himself the lowest and the servant of all. I hold myself amongst you as one who serves. I wash your feet that you may do the same for one another. If anyone gives you a blow upon one cheek turn the other to him. If anyone asks for your cloak give him your coat also. Resist not evil. I do not seek the glory of men.

My God, you have always so taught humility by word and example that you have made it one of your chief characteristics. You who were so great, teach me, who am so small and mean, to be humble like you. Your humility was to be an example for all men. You so comprehended the difference between the Creator and his creatures that you wished your human nature (though it made up one Person with your divine nature) to render the homage of an infinite humility to the Divinity, whose infinite grandeur you were able clearly to comprehend. So, if you chose to be humble, how much more should I be humble ; I, for whom S. Augustine said ' Humility is the truth,' should look upon myself as nothing, as a worm. Worse in some respects than the fallen spirits, not in all respects, but in that of having abused your grace and in having sinned innumerable times after having received your pardon.

For me indeed ' Humility is the truth.' Truth is for me to despise myself. I, who fall every day,

RETREAT AT NAZARETH

every hour, Truth for me is to think meanly of myself, of the baseness of my part and my present life, of the mean promptings of my spirit, I, who have so often deceived myself, to think of the weakness of my virtue which every day I see fail before the smallest temptation. I must be *humble in thought*, knowing myself and facing my own misery, past and present, the faults that I have, the virtues that I have not, the infirmities that I have and the natural gifts that I do not possess. I *must be humble in my desires*, without any ambition, or any wish for man's esteem, but desire on the contrary that they should know the truth and take me at my real value as a worm, as something proud, cowardly, obstinate and ungrateful. I must not indulge in day dreams (it is waste of time), especially in evil imaginations full of vanity and wordliness, inspired by ambition; I must be afraid of myself, afraid of my own judgement and integrity and courage. I must attribute to God only whatever good there may be in me, and to myself alone the evil I do.

Humble in speech. I must speak little, saying no good of myself, never revealing, unless under great necessity, all the graces God gives me; never saying anything which could give a good opinion of myself to others except under necessity. I must hide all that might give a good opinion of myself to others of my natural and supernatural gifts (though none come from myself, but all from God alone), I must hide any good that I may do if God does any through me. 'Let not your right hand know what your left hand doeth.' 'When you pray shut your door and let God alone see you.' I must speak humbly and gently and never give a proud answer to those who speak proudly to me; I must be humble and gentle with great or small whether I am reproached or praised, whether in prosperity or adversity; whether I be flattered or menaced I must be humble in speech and humble in the thought of death.

Humble in actions. I must believe no work beneath me, since Jesus was a carpenter for thirty years, and Joseph all his life. With this example I should, on the contrary, look upon any occupation or work as a great privilege. I must welcome with love and readiness any occasion for humility, any humiliation that emulates the humility of Jesus, and since if my sins were known to men nothing would seem to them bad enough for me, let me avoid all lofty occupations and all high positions because Jesus was lowly and despised. I must accept no promotion whatever it may be, unless only obedience imposes it on me and if I see that it is a duty and the will of God.

PRAYER

My Lord Jesus, to pray is to contemplate you, and since you are always there should I not contemplate you unceasingly if I love you truly? He who loves and is in the presence of the Beloved, can he do otherwise than gaze upon him? 'Teach us to pray,' so said the apostles. O my God, now is the time and the place. I am in my little hut, it is night and all sleeps around me, all is silent except the rain and the wind, and the crowing of the cocks in the distance reminding me of the night of your Passion. Teach me to pray, O my God, in this silence and recollection.

Yes, my child, you must pray without ceasing, pray whilst you work and read and study, as you walk and eat and sleep, you must have me always before your eyes, contemplating me unceasingly,

RETREAT AT NAZARETH

speaking to me when you can, your eyes always fixed on me.

Prayer is the familiar intercourse of the soul with God. It is nothing else. It is not essentially meditation or vocal prayer, but accompanies to a greater or lesser degree one or the other. Meditation is the thoughtful examination of some truth, or some duty which the mind seeks to understand at the feet of God. Meditation is always more or less mingled with prayer, for you needs must call God to your help from time to time to understand that which you meditate. Besides, you cannot stay so close to him for long without expressing any word of tenderness or love.

I am pleased when you say the Divine Office or your Rosary or the Stations of the Cross in my honour and I accept them with approval. They are an offering to me, a lovely and precious gift, though you, the giver, are so small. You are like a child that in my goodness I allow to pick the flowers in my garden, the best roses, so that, though you are so insignificant, you can gather a rare bouquet to offer me. I love to receive this offering from your hands, my beloved child, because, though you are so small and full of faults, you are my child and I love you. I created you to enjoy Heaven, my only Son bought you with his blood, and so made you doubly my child when he adopted you as his brother. I love you and you have heard my voice, and can repeat to yourself what I have said. 'If, when you knew me not I loved you so, now, poor and simple though you are, you seek to please me.' So you see, though I am great and you are small, though I am beautiful and you are ugly, though I am wise and you are ignorant, still I look for your daily offering, your flowers morning and evening ; I look for them and treasure them, for the roses I let you gather in my garden are so lovely and I prize them because I love you, though you are small and simple, my little child.'

Thanks, thanks, my God. Your words are sweet and full of light, and I see in them what I have not seen before. I thank you, my God. How good you are !

CHASTITY

My Lord Jesus, tell me what to think about this divine virtue. I have great need to learn of you, for I am so earthly, so smirched with the mud that I must needs be taught by you if I am to understand something of this heavenly virtue, I, who am so mean and sullied and earthly.

' My son, I was a virgin, and I chose a virgin as my Mother and as my foster father, my forerunner and as my favourite apostle. I ordained that in my Church in the Christian religion, my priests and those souls that consecrate themselves to me, should live in chastity. Virgins have their own special glory in Heaven.

' Few Saints have not from some special moment of their life, if not all through it, lived in chastity. For one who loves me truly and passionately, my love is a sacred tie like a marriage, and any thought or word or action contrary to chastity is an infidelity to the Spouse.'

Virginity or chastity, therefore, is not simply the unmarried state ; it is, on the contrary, the state of a soul married to the Beloved Spouse, to a perfect and holy and Beloved Spouse. ' Come and see how sweet is the Lord.' When we have seen that, how can we wish to live our life otherwise than in adoring him, in doing his will, far from the vanities of the world. All our time is taken up. We have seen the King of Kings. He has ravished our hearts for ever, we love him and have no wish for an earthly love. We have our Beloved and there is no room in us for two. We have looked into Heaven and are dead to the world. We would be God's alone; he suffices for our hearts; it is our hearts that do not suffice to give him all the love and worship that are due to him. We would not divide our affections, but be altogether his. We will love other men in his light, at his feet, as brothers, but we shall always be his and his alone, his alone.

' It is so little, my daughters, to belong to God,' said S. Teresa. We are Spouses, truly wedded Spouses because we wish it, and because we promise always to belong to him. How humble and good he is, he, the King of Heaven, to accept thus all these poor weak souls that offer themselves to him as Spouse. It is often difficult to find a mate on earth. How fleeting and passing, like dust and ashes, is an earthly union! it passes and falls to nothing. But he, the King of Heaven, one may have as one's Spouse when one will. He accepts every soul, however poor and despised, guilty or soiled, that offers herself to him with sincerity. He accepts them all and gives himself to all. My God, how good you are. In faith we live the life of the Spouse of Christ. By faith we live in Light, we know, we see. By faith we see that our souls are united to Jesus, that our lot is bound up in the Divine, that we are blessed, that our lives should be a perpetual Magnificat for our unbelievable happiness.

Our Lord speaks : ' You know, then, with what jealousy you must keep yourself from the least, the smallest, thought contrary to chastity, and still

MEDITATIONS OF A HERMIT

more from any word or act. This is essential to the fidelity that you owe to your Beloved, to the Spouse you love so passionately, and who, in his turn, loves you passionately. He has proved it in that he died for you, and gives you great graces. And now he takes your soul as his spouse for all time and eternity, in the shining light of Faith, and in the infinite joy of Heaven.'

Resolutions. To thank my Divine Spouse, very often, for the infinite grace he has given me in lighting me with the lamp of Faith, and letting me see what it is to be the Spouse of the King of Heaven. To thank him infinitely and constantly for having called and received me to be his spouse. He so great, I so small. To guard myself from the smallest, faintest failure, in thought, word or deed, in chastity, since such would be failure in the fidelity I owe my Spouse. For the love I bear him should make me abhor such a failure.

POVERTY

O my Lord Jesus, I now come to meditate on holy poverty. You must teach me about it, for you loved it much. Already in the Old Testament you took pleasure in it. In your human life you made it your faithful companion. You left it as a heritage for your Saints, and for all those who would follow you and all those who would be your disciples. You taught poverty by example all through your life. You glorified it, blessed it, proclaimed it necessary in your teaching. You chose poor workmen as your parents; you were born in a cave that was used as a stable; your childhood was poor and laborious. The first to worship you were shepherds. At your Presentation in the Temple,

RETREAT AT NAZARETH

your offering was that of the poor. Thirty years you lived as a poor workman, here in Nazareth, where in deep and ineffaceable joy I live the life of a menial, a dung carrier. Then during your public life you lived on alms amongst poor sinners that you took as your companions. 'Without a stone to lay your head upon.' At that time you told S. Teresa you slept in the open because you could find no roof to shelter you. On Calvary you were even stripped of your garments which remained your only possession, and the soldiers cast lots for them. Naked you died, and you were buried by the charity of strangers. 'Blessed are the poor.'

My Lord Jesus, he will soon make himself poor who loves you with his whole heart, for he will not bear to be richer than his beloved. My Lord Jesus, he will soon make himself poor who reflects that whatever is done for the least of your creatures is done to you, and whatever is withheld is denied to you, and so he will try to comfort all who come across his path. He will quickly make himself poor who takes your words in simple faith. 'If you would be perfect sell all you have and give to the poor.' 'Blessed are the poor, for whoever shall leave his possessions for me shall receive a hundredfold here and in heaven life eternal.'

My God, I know it is possible for some souls to see you poor and still to keep their own wealth, and thus to set themselves above their Beloved Master, and not wish to be like you in all things as far as they are able, above all in your abasement. I feel sure they love you, my God, but still I think there is something lacking in their love. In any case, for me it is not possible to say I love you without feeling an impelling desire to imitate you, and above all to share all the pains and the difficulties and hardships of your life. To me it is not possible, O my God, to be rich and at ease and enjoy a prosperous life, when you were poor, struggling, living laboriously. I cannot love thus. 'It is not right that the servant should be above his Master, nor that the Bride should be rich and the Bridegroom poor,' especially when he is voluntarily poor. S. Teresa, wearied with the importunities of those who wished her to accept endowments for her convent at Avila, was once almost ready to accept. But when she went to her oratory and saw the Crucifix she fell at the feet of Jesus, hanging naked on the Cross, and implored of him the grace never to let her receive any endowments, but always to be as poor as he was.

I judge no man, my God; all men are your servants and my brothers, and I must love them and succour them and pray for them. But for me, myself, it is impossible to understand loving without seeking to resemble the Beloved, and share his hardships. And again one gains so much. The poor man who has nothing loves no earthly things and is free. All is the same to him. It matters not to him where he is, where he may be sent. He has nothing and needs nothing anywhere. Everywhere he finds him from whom he expects all: God, who will give him always, if he is faithful, what is best for his soul. Only he is free. His spirit is light to rise to Heaven. There is no weight upon his wings. His thoughts are free from all earthly ties, and can fly freely to Heaven. Worldly things, great or small (for the small worries are as troublesome as the big ones), do not hinder his prayer. They do not exist for him. This is what you saw when you anointed Our Lord, blessed Mary Magdalen, and Our Lord has given you to me to teach me poverty,

RETREAT AT NAZARETH

perfect poverty, which is 'to possess nothing and use nothing that a poor workman would not use.'

This is the vow I have made in imitation of Jesus. But true poverty is more than this. True poverty is poverty of heart, which you said was 'blessed,' my Saviour Jesus, to which all material things are totally indifferent, for it has broken with them all. As S. Mary Magdalen broke her vase of spices, the heart empties itself utterly of all attachment to transitory things, it is left open wide for God alone. Then God enters in and reigns alone, filling it entirely, and makes subject for ever to himself, for him and in him, the love of all men, his children. The heart knows no other than these two loves; nothing else exists for it and we live on earth as though we were not there, in perpetual contemplation of the one necessity to our souls and in intercession for those that the Heart of Jesus loves.

ABJECTION

My Saviour Jesus, make this meditation for me. It was you who said, ' It is not meet that the servant should be above his Master.' By those words you command that I should not ever be set above you in the eyes of men. How can I practise this abjection?

'First notice that after I had said "the servant must not be above his Master," I added, "but he is perfect who is like to his Master." So it follows that though I do not expect you to be above what I was, I do not wish you to be lower. If there are exceptions to this you are certainly not one of them, for I have so often shewn you that your vocation is to imitate me. Try then to be, in the eyes of the world, just what I was at Nazareth, no more and

MEDITATIONS OF A HERMIT

no less. I was a poor workman, living by the work of my hands. I seemed to be ignorant, unlettered. My parents, relations and friends were poor artisans like myself or fishermen. I spoke with them as an equal, we dressed alike, we lived and ate alike. Like all poor men I was despised, and because I was, in the eyes of the world, only a " poor Nazarene," I was persecuted and ill-treated in my public life, so that, at my first words in the synagogue at Nazareth, they wanted to turn me out. In Galilee they called me Beelzebub, and in Judea they said I was a devil and possessed. I was treated as an impostor and a seducer, an ambitious usurper, and I was put to death on a gibbet between two thieves. Let yourself then, my child, be thought to be ignorant, poor, of low birth; indeed what you really are, without cleverness or talent or virtue; seek the lowest occupations, cultivate your mind in such measure as your director lays down for you, but let it be in secret and unknown to the world. I had infinite wisdom, but no one knew it. Fear not to study, it is good for your soul. Study zealously with the purpose of growing better, of knowing me better and living better. Also in order that you may resemble me, the Perfect Knowledge. Be very ignorant in the eyes of men and very wise in Divine Knowledge at the foot of my Tabernacle. I was lowly and disdained. Seek, ask for and love those occupations which degrade you, such as sweeping dung or digging the ground, whatever is most lowly and common; the more you make yourself lowly in these ways, the more you will be like me. Even if you are thought mad, all the better. Thank me infinitely. I was thought mad, that is a point of resemblance between us. If you should be stoned and reviled and cursed in the streets, all the

RETREAT AT NAZARETH

better. Thank me, for it is a great grace. Did they not do the same to me? You should rejoice that I make you like myself in this. But you must not bring this treatment upon yourself by eccentricity or strange behaviour; I did nothing to be so treated, I did not deserve it in any way, and yet I was so treated; so do nothing to deserve ill-treatment, but if I give you the grace to undergo it, thank me for it. Do nothing to prevent it or to stop it. Bear all with joy and gratitude that you should be given this gift from my brotherly hand. Act as I should have done. Do only good, but give yourself to the lowest, humblest task; shew yourself to others, by your dress, your lodging, your friendliness with the humble, to be the equal of the humblest. Hide carefully all that may exalt you in the eyes of your neighbour. But before me, in silence and solitude before the Tabernacle, study and read. You are alone, with door closed, with me and my Holy Parents, with Mary Magdalen. Unfold your mind and spirit at my feet, and do all that your director may prescribe for you to become better and holier, that you may the better console my Sacred Heart.'

MANUAL LABOUR

My God, shew me by your inspiration what is your Will with regard to manual labour.

'In this, as in humility and poverty, I require from you what I required from myself. You have a blessed vocation, my son, you are blessed indeed. Take me simply as your model. Do what you think I should do, never do anything I should not have done. Imitate me.

'Work then to earn your daily bread, but less

MEDITATIONS OF A HERMIT

than ordinary workmen do. They work to gain as much as possible ; you and I work only to earn a frugal livelihood, a humble lodging, and humble clothing and something over for alms. We need not work more because of our detachment from material things which makes us desire only the meanest in the way of lodging, clothing, and food, and of those only the merest necessities. We shall work less than ordinary labourers, because having less need of material comforts, we have, on the other hand, greater need of spiritual comfort, and we need more time for prayer, meditation and study.

' So it was in the house at Nazareth.'

In what manner should I work ?

' With your mind fixed always on me, my child. With this thought always present that you are working with me and for me, with Mary and Joseph, Mary Magdalen and our Guardian Angels.

' Contemplate me always with them.'

RETREAT

My God, help me, prompt me, aid me ; the more my retreat goes on the more I feel that I am powerless alone and how necessary it is that I should be inspired by you. Tell me, my God, in what retreat you would wish me to live.

' In that in which I lived my hidden life, my son, neither less nor more. My life was very retiring, was withdrawn from the world. Do not imagine that it was often that I and my Mother went to weddings. Remember that my Mother and S. Joseph had both embraced the perfect life of virginity, and that they lived in the world as not belonging to it. They were working people, but not just like others. If Judith willed to live out of the world in her dwelling, how much more did they. If all those who begin to love me leave the world and live more and more apart from it as their love increases, how much more did my holy parents live apart. When I began life I dwelt in this holy home, where our days were passed in contemplation, in fasting and prayer, and in work accompanied by prayer. Those holy souls had made out this life for themselves, for their conversation was in Heaven, they lived as brother and sister, and not as husband and wife, living for God only, apart from the world, alone, detached in the little town of Nazareth. I entered this life of theirs and took it upon myself. My presence drew Mary and Joseph still closer together; they were always together that they might always be with God, and more and more all other things than God became a burden to them. They hid their treasure between them, and shewed him not to profane eyes which would treat their God as a man. It was I who said " I am not of this world," and I inspired in them this love of retirement, and I inspire all souls with it as soon as they draw near to me. So I would choose no other life myself, and I entered into their quiet and hid myself in their solitude.

' He who loves, loves to dwell in solitude with the Beloved. He who loves God, loves to dwell in solitude at the feet of God. The Saints without exception loved solitude, for they all loved me, and he who loves me necessarily seeks to be alone with me. But he should love my glory and my honour still more, more than the joy of being alone with me, and as soon as my Will calls him here or there, he should fly to do it, and, leaving his solitude, throw his lot in amongst men. Then if my Will and

MEDITATIONS OF A HERMIT

my need no longer demand that he should mix with the world, he should obey the law of love and return to the desert. The more he loves the more he thirsts to be alone with me, the longer is he able to remain alone with me, and the more he leads a life of prayer.

' Until God called me to preach we remained thus in our solitude. Do not picture to yourself a family surrounded by affection, visited by friends and relatives. There was nothing of that for us. Ours was the life of two or three religious united in God, living together a life of recollection in a little solitary dwelling, a life of constant prayer and penances, of constant contemplation, the life of silence, the life of souls that do not belong to the world, who are wrapped up in God, whose conversation is in Heaven.'

So my life at Nazareth was a retreat. That is what yours should be. Live in recollection, in intercourse with God, at all moments of the day and as much as possible of the night; as seldom as possible, and only when necessary, leave your house. Stay out of it as short a time as you can. Salute all those you know. Shew a pleasant face to all, but speak with no one, unless it should be necessary, then say as little as you can, but always something kind and something that concerns God and leads to thoughts of him.

PENANCE

My Lord and my God, I need you to speak to me of Penance. Make me love it, shew me its beauty, make me see how inseparably it is bound up with your love, and then tell me what to do and finally help me to do it.

RETREAT AT NAZARETH

' My child, you have already spoken of penance, you have no need to be shewn its beauty. Is it not enough for you to know that I practised it all through my hidden life, that I practised it all through my public life as the gospel tells, that I fasted for forty days and died upon the cross? Is this example not enough to make you enter with all your strength into the spirit of penitence with no other motive than pure love and the simple need to imitate, to resemble me, to share my life and above all my sufferings? And if your love is so small that my example is not enough for you, you have my words: " Do Penance." " When the bridegroom is no longer with them they will fast." " This devil will not go forth save by prayer and fasting." And if my example and my words seem to you obscure, though really they are as clear as day, you have the example of my Saints. Every one, without exception, is a commentary, and should prove to you that I love and desire penance.

' Whenever you deny yourself anything, however small it may be, perhaps an impulse of curiosity, looking about you, eating an extra mouthful, driving away a fly, or refusing some small comfort, some small desire, the merest trifle, if you do it for love of me with the intention of offering me a sacrifice, you offer me an act of adoration and worship which pleases me and gives me great honour. All the more is it so when you sacrifice something which costs you more, a great humiliation, or some severe penance, a long vigil, or a vow that it costs much to observe.

' So you see how those who love me seek and desire to glorify me, by offering me this wonderful accumulation of honour, by doing such actions in a spirit of sacrifice, offering me from morning till

MEDITATIONS OF A HERMIT

night all sorts of mortifications, great and small. They have no need to preach or come out of their seclusion. It is enough that they deny themselves and suffer privations. Every minute of suffering endured for my name and offered to me, honours me and is a sweet-smelling sacrifice. Now you can understand the mortification of the saints and that desire for suffering of souls who hunger and thirst for my glory. You can understand how these souls that are full of zeal for the glory of God (mine more than any other) gave themselves to penance from morning till night at all hours to glorify God by this best of all offerings. This is what S. Paul means when he says : " I know only Jesus and Jesus crucified." All my life was voluntary suffering because all my life was a devouring desire for the glory of God. Penance is a very admirable means of glorifying him.'

Now do you understand why you must undertake penance? You must immerse yourself in it, but still always under obedience. It is not necessary that an act, to be a sacrifice, should be offered as one at the moment. It may have been offered as such beforehand, for all acts and all words and even all good thoughts may be offered to God as a sacrifice. It is not necessary to make a heap of sacrifices every day to God, and to think of them all day long, and to say to oneself every minute : ' Let me make a sacrifice.' It is enough to offer to God in a spirit of sacrifice and to his honour all our thoughts, words and actions of the day, our movements, our being, praying him that it may all make a sweet-smelling sacrifice to him. We shall thus be a perpetual victim and our sacrifice will last all through the day.

RETREAT AT NAZARETH

RECAPITULATION OF RESOLUTIONS

I must, with Jesus in the manger, embrace humility, poverty, detachment, abjection, solitude, suffering. I must make little of human greatness and the respect and approval of men, but I must respect the poor as much as the rich. For myself I must always seek the lowest of the low places, and arrange my life so that I may be the last and the most despised amongst men.

When I am sad, discouraged about myself and about others, I must think of Jesus in his glory, sitting on the right hand of the Father for ever, and rejoice. I should, at these times, say the glorious mysteries of the Rosary, so as to bathe my spirit in their joy.

Our Lord speaks. 'Never worry about small things. Break away from all that is small and mean, and try to live on the heights, not from pride, but from love.

'You must break with all that is not me. Make to yourself a desert where you will be as much alone with me as Mary Magdalen was alone in the desert with me. It is through detachment that you will attain to this, by driving out all mean thoughts, all littlenesses which are not evil in themselves, but which succeed in scattering your mind far from me, when you should be contemplating me from morning to night. Fix your mind on me as you work, as you pray ; contemplate me unceasingly and give all the time you can to prayer and holy reading, which will unite you to me and through which I will speak to you as I spoke to my parents and to Mary Magdalen at Nazareth and at Bethany. He who loves has his beloved always in his mind ; that

MEDITATIONS OF A HERMIT

time is to him well spent that is spent in contemplating him, and that time is to him wasted in which he is out of his sight. He counts as profitable only those hours in which he contemplates the only thing that to him has any reality. All else is for him emptiness and nothingness. Let your soul melt into mine, immerse yourself in me, lose yourself in me. Think of how often I have told you to hope for the day when you will lean for ever on my breast. And since I allow it I tell you now to begin to live this sweet life, in silence with Mary Magdalen and my Mother and S. Joseph, lay your head upon my breast and so accomplish your pilgrimage.'

I must never lose one chance, one single moment of being in the presence of the Blessed Sacrament, whatever may be the moral or material difficulties, or whatever danger or suffering must be faced in order to do so. The whole world is nothing beside my Master who dwells in the Tabernacle.

I must be humble in thoughts, words and acts. Never seek the approval of men, but love to be despised by them. He who loves is humble, because he feels small and mean beside his Beloved. He who loves imitates the Beloved, and Jesus was meek and humble of heart.

Humility is the crown of all virtues, and is necessary if we are to please God ; pride spoils all.

Ought I to cling to staying at Nazareth ? No, not more than to anything else. I should cling to nothing but the will of God. I should feel that it is a great grace to live at Nazareth, be happy in it and be grateful, but I should not attach myself to it. As soon as it is no longer the will of God that I should stay there, I should leave it instantly without hesitation, or a backward look, and go wherever his will calls me.

RETREAT AT NAZARETH

Our Lord speaks. 'One of the reasons for which I made myself poorer than the poorest working man is that I came to teach men to despise honours, that I came to teach men to despise worldly goods, and to give an example of complete poverty and deepest abjection. You have the same reasons as I, for it is part of your vocation to preach the Gospel from the housetops, not by word, but by your life.'

How can I pay God all I owe him, having received so much? By love, by obedience to all he asks of me (for obedience is a sign of love), by gratefully doing my duty, which is a part of perfect obedience. By two means in particular, which in the degree in which I offer them are a matter of counsel and not of command, but which are significant of love and of a burning heart. These two things are the fervent prayers which I offer daily as an offering of roses and flowers, and penance, the daily sacrifice, the sweet-smelling myrrh offered daily to embalm the Beloved. Prayer and penance must be the foundation of my life as they were that of Jesus at Nazareth, of Mary Magdalen at the anointing. I must take no pleasure for myself in ease of body; I can accept them for God's sake from him alone, because they may be the will of God, but not as a personal satisfaction. When God's will is not clearly shewn I must prefer penance, because it is a greater sacrifice to God. But before all things I must desire the will of God, for the best honour we can pay him is to do his will.

The purpose to offer God all possible sacrifices must not make me constrained and gloomy. I must have the holy liberty of the sons of God who cry 'Abba Pater' and be full of joy in God. I must never be held back by the natural fear that

MEDITATIONS OF A HERMIT

the devil always gives us at the beginning of all good works. 'He works through fear' and tries to turn us from all good and particularly from penance through fear. 'God loves a cheerful giver.'

A WEEK AT EPHRAIM

A RETREAT MADE IN 1898

From the Monday after the Third Sunday in Lent till the Monday after the Fourth Sunday in Lent

It is not known whether Charles de Foucauld really made this retreat at Ephraim, or whether, as he meditated alone, in his cell or in the chapel of the Poor Clares at Nazareth, he merely transported himself in spirit to Ephraim, listening to Our Lord's teaching as though he were living at the time of his Life in the world and were in his Master's presence with S. Mary Magdalen and the apostles. He is following in this the counsel of S. Ignatius : ' I will look in imagination upon the persons in the mystery I am meditating. I will place myself before them like a slave or a beggar, unworthy to come into their presence. I will watch them and contemplate them, and minister to their needs eagerly and respectfully, as though I were really with them. Then I will reflect upon the scene in my own mind and draw from it some profit to my soul.' (Spiritual Exercises of S. Ignatius.)

Second week. Monday, 3 a.m.

My Lord Jesus, I thank you for waking me, for calling me to watch with you between the Blessed Virgin and S. Mary Magdalen. How good you are ! Everything is still asleep in the house and without.

EIGHT DAYS AT EPHRAIM

Alone you watch with your Mother and your other faithful adorers. How good you are, my God, to call me to rise and watch with you and with them. I see you silent, kneeling. You pray to the Father, contemplating him, offering him those for whom you came on earth, those around you first, then all others present and future. Your Mother and Mary Magdalen are kneeling near you, very near, but so that they can see you, and they contemplate God through you. They never take their eyes off you. Silent they adore you in spirit, and their souls are immersed in you in love and endless adoration. Their hearts are torn between joy and sorrow. They feel the deepest happiness to be with you, alone with you, to possess you, to have you near in this silence and solitude, through hours of calm and peace and prayer. But sometimes a bloody vision passes before their eyes and they ask themselves sorrowfully, ' Where will he be a few days hence ? ' Between his executioners, bound, scourged and beaten, and a few hours hence all this beloved Body, which we adore so sweetly, will be nothing but a mass of blood. He will be nailed to a cross and he will die. And then your sorrow, O my Mother, O Magdalen, becomes deep as the sea ; your eyes fill with tears and you weep bitterly, you angels of peace. Oh ! my Mother, Mother of Perpetual Succour, and you, Mary Magdalen, set me between you during these long hours of vigil. Here is my soul, let it share in your feelings, your love, your joys and your sorrows ; do with it what you will ; I ask only one thing for it, do with it whatever can serve best to please Our Lord's Sacred Heart. I give myself up to you always, my beloved Mothers, let me comfort Our Lord at every moment of my life.

MEDITATIONS OF A HERMIT

O my God, thank you for letting me be at your feet! *Deficit anima mea.* How divinely good you are! You love me. It seems madness to think it. You, perfect God, love me, a poor, evil, cowardly creature, falling a thousand times a day. No, it is not madness, it is truth, the truth of your Divine Heart, and your love is far beyond our love and your heart far beyond our hearts. Yes, it is true, you love me in spite of my nothingness and misery. You have told us so ; that is enough. But even if you had not told me so, the mere fact of waking me and calling me to watch with you between your Mother and Mary Magdalen would prove it to me. O my God, how good you are and how happy am I. My God, I love you, I adore you. Let me, with your Mother and Mary Magdalen, lose myself and sink myself in love and contemplation of you.

8 a.m.

We are still around you, Blessed Virgin, Mary Magdalen, the apostles and this wretched unworthy creature whom you allow to be at your feet. The room is closed, not a sound from without but the sound of rain. You open your lips and you speak, my God. We all look at you, we listen to you with living attention. You say that you have still eight days to pass at Ephraim. You will leave next Tuesday, a week hence, and go to Galilee. There you do not stay long, for on Friday fortnight you will be at Bethany, and Friday, three weeks hence, the day of Sacrifice of the Passover, will be also the day of the Sacrifice of the Lamb of God. You say that during the eight days of this retreat you are going to survey the chief acts of your life with your children around you. You are the Truth and the Life. In your Sacraments and your grace, you will ever be the Life of souls,

EIGHT DAYS AT EPHRAIM

and you will pour this Life freely into them. As to the Truth and the Way, you have shewn these to us through all the thirty years of your life, and you will still shew them here on earth till the Ascension. But then all will be over. The world must live on memory till the end of time. Your teaching, you say, and your example, are at the same time the Way and the Truth.

THE INCARNATION

Our Lord speaks. ' See in the Incarnation *Love for all men*, God's love for them, and see that you have the same love through his love in order that you may be perfect as your heavenly Father is perfect. How deep this love is, how active and living! It bridges over the distance which separates the finite and the infinite, and through this love he uses the Incarnation, that unbelievable external means for our salvation. He, God, the creator, comes to live upon earth.'

Our Lord speaks. ' Look at my devotion to men and see what yours ought to be. Look at this act of humility for the sake of man's welfare and learn to humble yourself for the good of souls, giving yourself first to them as I did. Lowering yourself to gain others, not fearing to humble yourself or to set your rights aside when there is a question of doing good to souls. Never think that in lowering yourself you have less power for good. On the contrary, in thus humbling yourself you are imitating me and using the same means that I used. You are walking in my *Way*, and therefore in the *Truth*, and you are in the right state to receive *Life* and impart it to others. The best means for this is always to imitate me. I came down to the level of men by my Incarnation, and to that of sinners by my Circumcision and Baptism. Be lowly, lowly, humble, humble. Let those that are in high places put themselves last in a spirit of lowliness and service, love for men, humility, taking the lowest place so long as the divine will does not call you to another, for in that case you must obey. Obedience first of all—conformity to the will of God. If you are placed high, then keep yourself in humility of soul as though you were the last ; occupy your high position as though you were there only to serve others and to lead them to salvation, and as if, though you may command them, you are rather serving them, for you command them only with the purpose of sanctifying them.'

MEDITATION ON THE VISITATION

Gospel according to S. Luke i, 39.

'Very soon after my Incarnation I made my Mother take me to the home where John was to be born that I might sanctify him before his birth. I gave myself to the world in the Incarnation for his sanctification. Even before my birth I was busy with my great work, the sanctification of men, and I urged my Mother along to work with me. Not only her did I urge along to sanctify others as soon as she possessed me, but I do so to all other souls to whom I give myself. Some day I shall say to my apostles : " Preach," and I shall shew them their mission and trace out their rules. Here I say to other souls, to all those who possess me and lead a hidden life, who possess me but have not yet been given a mission to preach, I say to these, let them sanctify souls by carrying me in silence amongst them ; to silent souls, living a hidden life, away from the world and in solitude, I say : " Work, all of you, for the sanctification of the world ; work for it like my Mother, silently, without words ; go amongst those who know me not and there establish your silent retreats. Take me into their midst and set up my altar and the Tabernacle. Take to them the Gospel, but preach it by example rather than by word, rather by living it than preaching it ; sanctify the world, all you devout souls, hidden and silent, as Mary did when she carried me to S. John." '

5 *p.m.*

The time passes, my God, the hours go by, another day done and the evening come. Alas ! You have few days left here below. There are few days left to pass at your feet. In twenty-five days where will you be at this hour ? Alas, my God, you will live no more ! Gone out of life in suffering and pain. For us alone you came here below. Men would not receive you at your Birth and they expel you from the world in cruel torment. Thus did the world receive its God, its Saviour and Creator. True, you leave the world to enter into your glory, and it is very right that you should cease to be the Man of Sorrows to become the King of Glory. But, my God, through what overwhelming torments must you pass before you take your place at the right hand of the Father. When you came into the world no one would receive you, all the doors were shut to you at Bethlehem, and hardly were you born when they pursued you to put you to death. All the thirty years that followed you could find peace only by living a hidden life, either in foreign lands or in your little village, hidden away in the mountains, buried in silence and

MEDITATIONS OF A HERMIT

abjection. As soon as you came out of this silence you were persecuted. Your own fellow-townsmen first of all sought to put you to death ; all through the three years of your preaching you were menaced by death from all quarters, and now the menace is to be realized. Thus the world received its God. Yet you did not reject it but you blessed it when you left it. Every day you bless it ; a million times every day till the end of time. You overwhelm it with graces, you have returned to it, and will dwell in it for ever, not only in one place, but in many places. But now is the hour of parting. My God, I thank you that I am at your feet ; I thank you for this grace, that you let me share, with the Blessed Virgin, Mary Magdalen and your holy apostles, your last retreat, your last journeys and your last days.

THE NATIVITY

> Gospel according to S. Luke ii, 7. And she brought forth her first-born son and wrapped him up in swaddling clothes and laid him in a manger : because there was no room for them in the inn.

' I was born, born for you, born in a cave, in December, in the cold, forsaken, on a wintry night, in poverty, unknown even to the poorest, in solitude and abandonment. What do I teach you, my children, in this birth ? *To believe in my love*, since I have loved you thus far ; to hope in me, since I love you. I teach you to despise the world that is so little to me. I teach you poverty, abjection, solitude, humility, penance. I teach you to love me, for I am worthy of love. It did not satisfy my tender love to give myself to the world in the Incarnation and to sanctify it secretly in the Visitation. Ever since my Birth I have shewn myself to you and have put myself entirely in your hands. Ever since then you have been able to see me, hold me, hear me, serve me, console me. Love me, love me, for I am close to you. I give myself generously to you, and I am worthy of Love. In my great goodness I did not give myself to you just at my Birth for a few days or years, but I gave myself into your hands for ever, till the end of time. Think of the blessings I have given you in my Birth, that you can *serve me*, serve me in serving the Church, serve me in serving your neighbours, serve me, living there near me in the Tabernacle. You can not only serve me but you can console me. I lived every experience of your life in my life, and my human heart, which loves you so much, rejoiced and suffered with you in all these experiences ; rejoiced if they were directed to good, suffered if they were directed to harm. How blessed for you to be able to console me every moment of your life.

'I became for you a little gentle, tender child. Be not afraid of me ; come, take me in your arms and adore me, caress me as a child loves to be caressed. See, I hold out my arms to you. Be not afraid to caress me, a little tender babe. I am your God, but I am gentle and smiling. Be not afraid, but full of tenderness and love and confidence. And obedient, obedient not directly to God, but *indirectly*, by obeying in his sight those whom he has given you as teachers, parents, superiors or directors. Superiors of all sorts, each in the measure in which God has told you to obey.'

MEDITATIONS OF A HERMIT

THE CIRCUMCISION

S. Luke ii, 21. And after eight days were accomplished, that the child should be circumcised, his name was called Jesus, which was called by the angel before he was conceived in the womb.

'It was my will to be circumcised and to take the name of Jesus, Saviour. It was my will to put myself on the level of sinners to teach you *humility*. Look and see, my children, how all my acts teach humility. You need to learn this virtue and to practise it every day of your life. By pride the angels were lost and by pride Adam fell. You will always be tempted by pride; build your foundations upon humility; there is your salvation. Have I not given you a thousand examples of this? My Incarnation shewed infinite, unbounded humility. My Birth was humility. All in me is humility. I am gentle and humble of heart.

'In my Circumcision I teach also obedience: perfect obedience to all the laws of the Church, great or small; obedience without question or discussion, or any thought of personal advantage, obedience for obedience' sake.

'I teach also penance and love. Penance in that I undertook the pain; love, in that, on the eighth day of my life, I shed blood for you.

'It was my will to be called Jesus. First, because this is truth, the truth that you should love so much; then because it has so sweet a meaning and expresses so well my meaning for you; finally because it should inspire confidence in me, and

EIGHT DAYS AT EPHRAIM

should make you hold out your hand to me as one does to one's rescuer, to turn to me always with perfect confidence. This is what I want from you. Again and again I have called myself your Father and shewn myself to be one. Whilst you adore me as your God I ask from you the love of a son and a brother, and utter reliance and confidence.'

THE HIDDEN LIFE

> S. Luke ii, 39. And after they had performed all things according to the law of the Lord, they returned into Galilee, to their city Nazareth.

'After my Presentation and after the Flight into Egypt, I retired into Nazareth and there I lived all my childhood and my youth till my thirtieth year. This again I did for you, for love of you. What is the life I led? I led it for your instruction. All through those thirty years I was teaching you, not by words but by silent example. What is it that you should learn from it? First you will learn that good, great good, infinite, divine good can be done silently, quietly, without words or noise, by a good example. What example? That of piety, of loving fulfilment of duty, of kindness to all around one, of goodness to all near, of home ties faithfully observed. An example of poverty, hard work, abjection, recollection, retirement, of obscurity in a life hidden in God, of a life of prayer and penance and retirement, a life lost and immersed in God. You will learn to live by the labour of your hands, that you may be a burden on no one, and may have something to give to the poor, and I give to this manner of life an incomparable beauty in that you can imitate me in it.

'All who would be perfect should live *poorly*, in faithful imitation of my poverty at Nazareth. I taught *humility* at Nazareth by living there those thirty years a hidden life as an obscure workman; for all the thirty years that I spent there, unknown to all, I, the Light of the world, I taught *obedience* because I was subject to my parents all those thirty years; though they were good and holy, they were human and I am God. Seeing me obedient so long to those to whom I owed no obedience since I was their Sovereign Master, Creator and Judge, how can you refuse perfect obedience to those of whom I have said : " He who hears them hears me " ?

'I shew contempt of human things, of human greatness, of worldly standards, of all that the world approves, birth, riches, rank, science, cleverness, reputation, respect, worldly distinction, fine manners. All such things I reject, so that in me you find only a very poor workman, living devoutly in great obscurity.'

MEDITATION ON THE TEMPTATION OF OUR LORD IN THE DESERT

S. Luke iv, 12. Thou shalt not tempt the Lord thy God.

'I let the devil tempt me in the desert for you, for love of you and for your instruction; that you might know in the first place that there is greater temptation in the desert than elsewhere and that those who, for love of me, choose the solitary life, must be neither surprised nor discouraged by the multiplicity of its temptations; further that you should understand that temptation is not sin, since

EIGHT DAYS AT EPHRAIM

I myself was tempted, and tempted by monstrous things. Therefore you should neither be distressed nor discouraged when you are tempted, nor ever despise or blame your brother when he is tempted; and finally that you may see how to resist temptation. It must be resisted at once, as soon as it appears, from the first instant. A good way to fight temptations is to confront them with words of Holy Scripture which draw divine strength from their source.'

Wednesday, 3 a.m.

Thank you, my God, for waking me and rousing me from sleep. O my God, in the sadness and heart-tearing of the last days, the only consolation is to be constantly at your feet, to contemplate you unceasingly. But I would rather forget my own consolation, my God, and do nothing for it, but rather only for yours. Your consolation, my God, is that your children should be around you as much as possible. You say to us, if not to all, at least to many, and certainly to me (and how much I thank you for this), ' Watch and pray with me.' Holy Virgin, S. Mary Magdalen, give me place between you at the feet of Our Lord. Let me contemplate him and pray to him with you. Keep alert my eyes, my mind, my heart. Everything sleeps without. Here Jesus is before us. He prays, adoring his Father. He prays for men. He looks at us from time to time, gently, encouragingly, but always praying. My God, I adore you. Let me pass this early morning, this day and all my nights and days in love and contemplation. O my God, you are there before me. What will you that I think or that I say to you out of the depths of my heart?

MEDITATIONS OF A HERMIT

'I do not ask you to think a great deal, but to love a great deal,' the Holy Spirit answers. 'Adore me, love me, contemplate me ; tell me and repeat over and over again that you love me, that you give yourself to me, that you long for all my children to give themselves to me and love me.'

All is sleeping, all is at rest. Thank you, my God, for calling me to adore you and love you. Hold my eyes open and set wide the gates of my soul. Let me lose and sink myself in the contemplation and love of you.

S. Luke iv, 42. And when it was day, going out he went into a desert place : and the multitude sought him and came unto him. And they stayed him that he should not depart from them.

Our Lord speaks. 'In this manner did I spend the three years of my public life before the eyes of men. My days were spent wholly in teaching and healing, in doing good to men's souls and to their bodies too. And in the evening I withdrew from the crowd to whom I gave myself up all day, and seeking solitude I would shut myself away in some hospitable home, or I would go up into the mountains to some deserted and solitary place and pass the night in prayer. Always I spent the night in quiet recollection and silence, away from the crowd. This example I leave you. It was for you that I acted thus. I am strong enough and independent enough to be always as though alone with my Father, for I see him always and am always in his presence, and I have no need really of solitude in which to pray to him, nor silence to be united to

EIGHT DAYS AT EPHRAIM

him, nor for special prayers in which to speak to him. In the midst of the multitude I am as much united to him as in complete solitude. I have no need to meditate upon him to know him, for I know him already. I have no need to strengthen myself by contemplating him, for I am strong in my Divinity. I have no need of solitude or watchings or silence or prayer, for prayer is continued and perfect within me. Therefore it is for your example that I passed so many nights in solitary watching, praying to my Father, under the starry sky or in the secret cell. Since I do all for you all, love me and love one another. And follow my example. Sleep the least you can and pass all the time you can of the night in watching, in silence and recollectedness, praying, contemplating, sinking yourself in God.'

OUR LORD DEFENDS HIS DISCIPLES

S. Luke v, 32. I came not to call the just, but sinners to penance.

' Remember, my children, how I defended you whenever the Pharisees attacked you or tried to confuse you by their questions and arguments. Do you the same. Protect the good against the bad, the weak against those that treat them unjustly. I defended you for love of you and love of all men, for love of you personally, to constrain you to love me out of gratitude and to love your neighbour, imitating what I did to save you from evils that menaced, from dangers that approached, to give you an example and teach you to defend your children, your spiritual sons, all that are innocent and oppressed, as I defended you. Have I ever failed in this duty of defending those that are oppressed? I never have and I never shall till the end of time. I defend those that are falsely accused even against you who are my friends; I defend Mary Magdalen against her sister. I am faithful and I never see my friends attacked without taking up arms for them. Do you the same; it is a work of charity, one of the signs of the love you should bear to your neighbour.'

Thursday, 3 a.m.

Oh, how sweet to be at your feet, between the Blessed Virgin and Mary Magdalen, amongst your holy apostles. They too have risen to watch silently, contemplating you and praying. The hours pass and you pray still. You contemplate your Father and you pray for your children. It is short, this prayer, for it is always heard and is all-powerful. Your Father listens to your prayer always; he does all you ask, for you ask only what he wills; a word is enough for your petition. You lay your prayer before him by a simple movement of the soul, praying with few words, for he grants all you ask and you are one with him. But your contemplation is long and your act of Love is slow. All Eternity is not enough for you to adore and love. The eternal ages are filled with your love and adoration, so the hours of one night are nothing and pass like a flash in this heavenly work. You contemplate God, sometimes kneeling, sometimes sitting; from time to time your look passes tenderly over those children of God who press round you, and over their Guardian Angels who adore you. You contemplate God; Mary Magdalen and the apostles contemplate him too in contemplating you. Their eyes never leave their Beloved. They pray in silence, their eyes fixed upon you, you, their All. Your

EIGHT DAYS AT EPHRAIM

sweet pale face is feebly lit by the dim light of a little lamp. Their eyes are fixed on you, and they are lost in silent contemplation, sunk at your feet without other thought, contemplating and adoring you with loving hearts. To some comes sadness as they look upon you, thinking in their hearts, ' How long, Jesus beloved, blessed God, dear Master, have we got you still amongst us? How many more nights shall we pass thus at your feet in sorrowing prayer? In three weeks at this time you will have but one day and a half to live. What grief and sorrow to think that he will leave this world in cruel torments; this world that would not receive him, that rejected him, that had nothing to offer him but persecutions all his life. O my God, you have so many executioners and enemies. Let your few friends at least be faithful to you, let them be courageous, ardent in their service, steadfast in doing your will, in doing your pleasure, and ready to do all for your love and your service.

OUR LORD HEALS THE MAN WITH A WITHERED HAND ON THE SABBATH

S. Luke vi, 10. And looking round about on them all, he said to the man : stretch forth thy hand. And he stretched it forth. And his hand was restored.

Jesus speaks. ' Remember the *courage* with which in the midst of my enemies, whilst they were actually plotting to take me, I proclaimed aloud to their faces the true doctrine and truths that I knew to be the most odious and insupportable to them. Remember the courage with which I did these miracles and cures in their very midst, acts which filled them with rage and made them swear to put me to death. All this I said for you, to give all men a lesson of *courage* in practising charity, and in carrying out their religious duties, and to the shepherd of souls especially—courage to preach. Never hide the truth, whatever it may cost you : if it costs you martyrdom all the better : you will reign the sooner with my Father in Heaven. But remember my example. I am the Light and I have not the right to put myself under a bushel : I must be a Light to all men, even in spite of themselves, until my Father strikes the hour of my repose. You too who minister to souls, I have set you up as shining lights. It is your duty to enlighten men, whether they wish it or no ; it is your duty to sow the seed that I have given you to sow, to cry from the rooftops the truth that I have spoken to your ears. Cry out, sow, preach ! do it in obedience to me. Do it with joy, which is sweetened again by the thought that in obeying me you are imitating me. Whether you are heard or not, preach still, and pray always that your words may bear some fruit. If they bear none, go on all the same and be neither disappointed nor discouraged, and pray always that your words may bear fruit, be glad in a way for your failure, for in this too you share my lot.'

THE BEATITUDES

' " Blessed are they who are poor in spirit," who have not only given up their worldly goods, which is the first step, but rise much higher, emptying their souls of all attachment, taste, desire, or search for anything that is not me. Such poverty of spirit makes an empty space in the soul, clearing from it all love of oneself, driving out all human and material attachment and leaving a wide empty place that I fill up entirely. When that is done, then I give back to them, divinely transformed, this love for material things which they drove out of their hearts that I might fill it. These affections once driven from their hearts, I fill their souls now empty of all save me. Then in me, in my sight, they will begin once more to love these things, not for themselves or their own enjoyment, but for my sake in true Charity. They will love all creatures for me and none for themselves, for they owe me all their love, they must lose themselves in me and own nothing but by me and for me and their love like the rest. Blessed are they that are poor in spirit, empty of all, full of me.

' " Blessed are they who hunger." They who hunger for righteousness, for the reign of righteousness upon earth, for my glory ; hunger to see me glorified by all souls, hunger to see my will done perfectly by all creatures. This is the hunger that drives my own heart. Hunger like this, and more and more, not for your own sake or for human regard, but for God and love of God. You will be blessed then, for you will be perfectly united to my Sacred Heart.'

' Blessed are they who weep because they are suffering, poor, sick, mourning, suffering in body or mind, tried in some manner or other. They are blessed because such suffering will expiate their sins in some measure ; blessed because these sufferings help to detach them from the world and from earthly things, and make them raise their eyes to me and cling to me. Still more blessed are those who weep for their own sins, and yet more blessed are they who weep for my pain and Passion and all

MEDITATIONS OF A HERMIT

the sufferings I endured on earth. But the happiest of all are they who weep for pure love, who weep because they love me, not for any special reason, not for grief or desire, but just because when they think of me their hearts melt and they cannot restrain their tears.'

'Blessed are they whom men hate and persecute because of me. They are blessed because they imitate me and share my lot. Like true spouses they share the fortunes of the Bridegroom. Blessed are they, for what is sweeter than to suffer with those one loves. They are happy because they have the double joy of suffering with their Beloved and suffering for him, and blessed because in suffering thus their love for me grows greater; it grows in measure with that which they suffer for my sake, and this growing love will not pass away but will last in time and eternity. Oh, how blessed are they who suffer persecution with me and for me, and whose love grows all through these persecutions. Never fear, never refuse, to suffer pain or hatred or persecution for my sake. Accept them with joy, blessing and thanksgiving, with gratitude to God and man; thank me from the depths of your heart. Pray for your enemies and your persecutors, uniting yourselves like earthly angels to their Guardian Angels to pray for their conversion, and rejoice with all your hearts that you have been thought worthy to suffer humiliation and reproach for love of me. Never forget that it is thus that I treat all those whom I single out for my special love. Thus did I treat the Patriarchs and the Prophets, and thus I treated my Mother and my dear S. Joseph, and thus S. Mary Magdalen and Peter, John and James, all of whom I loved much. Thus above all do I serve myself, I who am first in all things. And

EIGHT DAYS AT EPHRAIM

how blessed shall be the end of this pain. The more you have loved and suffered for me in this world, the more you have been persecuted for me, so much the better will you see me and love me eternally in the next.'

5 *p.m.*

'Speak, Lord, your servant heareth.' Here between the Blessed Virgin and S. Mary Magdalen, your apostles all around us, I am here, humble, abject, I look upon you and listen for your words.

'Love your enemies. Bless those that curse you. Do good to those that do you harm. If anyone should strike you on one cheek offer him the other. If he take your cloak offer him also your coat. Give to all who ask of you. And if anyone should take something from you, ask him not again for it. Do to others as you would have them do to you. Be merciful as your Heavenly Father is merciful. Judge not and you shall not be judged. Forgive, and God will forgive you. Regard not the mote in thy brother's eye, but take heed to the beam that is in thine own eye.'

'All these commandments are about Charity, my children, and they will not surprise you when you understand, once for all, that all men together make up one family with God as their Father, Creator, Saviour, Father of all in the same manner. He loves all men incomparably more than the most tender father can love his children. And he wishes that amongst his children and amongst all the faithful there should reign perfect concord and love and tenderness, and, if needed, a sweetness ever ready to yield, such as a father loves to see between his children. This is how he would have us yield to each other ; help each other without calculation,

MEDITATIONS OF A HERMIT

give up each our own rights and never think of exacting them, giving way to an unjust brother so as to correct him by gentleness, keeping peace in the family, only praying for him that he may correct himself. So you see all these recommendations I give you are all to the same end, to keep peace and love amongst the brothers who make up my vast human family. Always observe these precepts and keep engraved deeply in the depths of your soul this principle from which all others spring, that all men are truly, really, brothers in God, their common Father, and God wishes them to love each other as such and treat each other in all things with brotherly love.

'And be compassionate one for the other: see my compassion for you, how I pity, suffer and condole with all sufferers, how I sigh with this one and weep with another. I feel for them in their mourning, their sickness, their anxieties, their hunger, their weakness, their ignorance; I help their souls and their bodies, and my Sacred Heart has deep pity and compassion for all their troubles of soul and body. Compassion is part of love in every human heart.'

THE CALMING OF THE TEMPEST

'My children, whatever happens to you, remember that I am always with you; remember whether you perceive me or not, whether I seem to be active or sleeping, forgetful of you, I am always watching and am always all-powerful. Never be afraid, never be anxious: I am there. I watch, I love. You never doubt my love, I hope. I am all-powerful. What more do you ask? All that happens to you is by my permission and will, by

EIGHT DAYS AT EPHRAIM

my loving will, that you may draw good out of it, good that I myself, through my grace, help you to derive from it. Therefore, fear nothing, since nothing can happen to you that is not permitted by me. Be not troubled (unless it be by instinctive feelings that involuntarily rush over you, prompted by nature and the senses) but unite your will with mine. Remember how many storms I have quieted by a word, making a great calm to follow. Remember how I held up Peter walking on the waters. I am always as near to all men as I was then to him, and as ready to help and succour in all that is for the good of the soul. Be confident, faithful, courageous ; have no fear for your body and soul, for I am there, loving and all-powerful. But forget not that I am there. Let not your confidence make you careless or neglectful of the dangers or confident in yourself or in others, for your position is very grave ; you have few years left, a few days, in which to gain a blessed Heaven or to merit eternal Hell. You are in imminent danger. Evil spirits, those strong and crafty enemies, your own human nature, the world, make perpetual warfare upon you. You must have no confidence in yourself. Look back in mind at your sins through the years and this survey will shew you what sort of foundations you can make of your own virtues and strength and character. No more can you count upon others ; they can neither act for you, nor can they help you without your consent, and without me they are as impotent as you. In this life the tempest never ceases, and your boat is ever ready to sink. But I am there, and with me it will never be wrecked. Trust nothing, yourself least of all ; but in me have that perfect confidence that banishes fear.'

MEDITATIONS OF A HERMIT

8 p.m.

My God, now the silent hour has returned. Night wraps the earth, the sky is black with clouds, no sound to be heard but a distant singing. How sad is the sound of this song that comes, borne by the wind, from some worldly haunt of men. What a false note it sounds! It is that cry from the heart of man that tries to be joyous but, in spite of itself, because it is not sanctified by you, my Saviour, is very plaintive. It is the true expression of human pleasures; the more one tries to find joy in them, the more they seem filled with tears. Oh, how blessed are we, my Saviour, Jesus, to be so far from this sad dull world, whose echoes reach us faintly on the wind. How good to draw close to you, in this little room, between your Mother, Mary Magdalen and the apostles, contemplating you, listening to you, and as the night goes on, staying silent at your feet, between these holy souls, losing myself with them in contemplation.

My Lord and my God, where will you be in three weeks from to-day? At this hour you will eat your last supper; at this hour you will be within a short space of your Agony, of your arrest. O my God, let me spend this night in such a way that it may console you, for in three weeks at this same hour you will be in great sorrow and suffering.

THE MULTIPLYING OF BREAD

S. Luke ix, 16.

Our Lord speaks. ' My little children, remember that amongst all the miracles that I did before your eyes some had a special character. They were the symbol of a great mystery. I explained to you as

EIGHT DAYS AT EPHRAIM

well as to the crowd something of this mystery at Capernaum, and these truths so surprised men that the greater number of them did not believe me, and many of my disciples left me and ceased from that day to follow me. Now I would speak of the Multiplying of the Bread which prefigured the Sacrament of my Body and Blood which I instituted on the eve of my Death and at the last hour and the Last Supper. I cannot bear, my children, to part with you altogether. I would not leave you orphans. I shall leave you in three weeks at this same hour, but soon I shall return to you, first between my Resurrection and my Ascension, and then afterwards in the Blessed Sacrament of the Altar until the end of time. Thus, though I rise into Heaven I remain on earth, and I shall be with you until the consummation of the world. I do this to make you, who are cold, become warm, fervent, loving, tender, by my presence, by the sight of me and of my love. You who are weak I make strong and courageous by the sense of my presence, by the clear knowledge that I am always with you; you, who are without hope and confidence, I make you hopeful and confident by the knowledge of my love for you, my friendship for you. You who are sad and discouraged I make happy, joyful, full of cheer, by the joy of being at the feet, the knees of your Beloved, ever in his presence. You who are full of material, external, worldly things, passing things that concern only your bodies, I constrain to leave these aside and concern yourself only with spiritual, interior, heavenly, eternal things, things of the soul. I draw you to the Church by my presence, I make you pass your days at the foot of my altar, for the love of my presence. I constrain you to pray to me whom you feel so near to you in the Tabernacle, to pass whole days in contemplation before the Sacred Host, for you know it to be truly me, the Lord that you love. This is not all ; when I give you this heavenly Bread I offer myself not only for your adoration, though my presence alone would be an infinite, a divine and complete and perfect gift, but I give you also through my presence in your tabernacles till the end of the world, not only this infinite gift, but two others also infinite : these are the gift of your food and nourishment, and also the sacrifice of myself that you can offer to my Father in my name.'

GENTLENESS

S. Luke ix, 56.

'Another virtue that I have often urged you to practise by word, and still more often by example, is gentleness. How often have I preached it for your good ! Practise this gentleness in your thoughts, thrusting out all bitterness of thought as inspired by the devil, all hardness and stiffness and insolence and anger, all hatred and stern judgement of others for whom you are not responsible. Welcome and nourish gentle, tender, charitable thoughts, thoughts of sympathy and goodness and gratitude. Soften your hearts with the thought of the love you owe to all men, to your brothers, who are my beloved children. Think what gratitude you owe them for the benefit we all receive from each other from the Communion of Saints, from the glory they lend me whether they will or no, to me, your Well-beloved. All men are tender friends and true to you, because they have at their side their Guardian Angels. Keep your thoughts sweet,

EIGHT DAYS AT EPHRAIM

tender and peaceful. And keep your words so too. If sometimes duty obliges you to rebuke, let there be seen under your severity, as though through a thin veil, a depth of eternal gentleness. Shew that the severity is only passing and will be withdrawn as soon as those souls, for whose good it is evoked, need it no longer and that it asks only to vanish and give place to sweetness.'

THE GREATEST COMMANDMENT

'Often, my children, they have asked me in your presence what is the greatest commandment, and I have always replied, the first commandment is to love God with all your heart and all your soul and all your strength, the second is to love your neighbour as yourself.

'What does it mean to love me thus, my children? It means to love me as your King, above everything, as much as you can, as much as the grace I give you makes it possible to love me. What does loving mean? It means many things which vary with different characters and with the various gifts of God. God gives sometimes one aspiration and sometimes another. To one soul he may give this feeling, to another that feeling. In the same soul he may at one time give one inspiration and at another time quite another, and these in very different degrees of intensity. All these different sentiments are united in love and are the real effects of love, but we feel them more or less according to God's will and to his grace and to our faithfulness in receiving this grace. Amongst these innumerable sentiments which all have their share in love, the first and foremost is the longing to see, to know, to possess the Beloved; the longing

MEDITATIONS OF A HERMIT

to be loved by him, the longing to please him, to do him some good; the desire to praise him, admire him, imitate him; the desire to be approved by him, to obey him in everything, to see him pleased, to see him possessed of all that is good and to his glory; the longing, in a word, for all that is for his good; the wish to suffer for him, to share his labours, his life, his conditions; to conform one's soul entirely to him; the wish to give oneself to him, to live only for him, and that every breath may be for him; the longing to labour for his service, to share the pain of his sufferings, the joy of his joy, the pain of those things that grieve him, and in union with him to rejoice in those things that please him. All these sentiments are the effect, result, outcome of love. They belong to love and are part of love, but they are not all love itself. A single one of them is really the essence of love—that is to desire passionately and above all things the well-being of the Beloved, to that degree that all else means nothing to one, that one lives only for the accomplishment of this desire.

'I have told you that the second commandment is to love one's neighbour as oneself. Now to love me perfectly you have emptied your soul, you have left nothing in it of material things, neither your neighbour nor yourself have any place in it. You have given all its space to me and I reign there alone, filling it entirely. But when once you let me reign fully and entirely in you, I establish myself in your soul and I put into it all that I wish to see there, just as a householder puts the furniture he needs into his house. I put into it my virtues, my goodness, and the first thing I bring into it and what I desire above all to see in it and what I wish you to cherish for me, for my use, in obedience to me, for my sake, in this house of your soul that you have given over to me, is love for all men. Equal love for all, for yourself and for others. For you are mine. Feel very great love for all (for yourself as much as all the others) because you are all so dear to me. Have I not proved it, my children, by all the graces showered upon men since the beginning of the world and by the incomprehensible grace of the Incarnation, by my whole life and above all by what I still can give and suffer for you, my beloved children, my heart's children?'

Saturday, 9 p.m.

My God, now the night has fallen. The wind has blown up into a storm, now and again the rain joins in. All other sounds are silent, only the wind is to be heard blowing and the rain falling. You are praying still and silent, a little lamp lights your face, beautiful, calm, thoughtful. Near you the Holy Virgin, S. Mary Magdalen, are on their knees praying. Your apostles are there too, silent, recollected, praying. All contemplate; their eyes never tire of looking upon you. Put me amongst them, my God, at your feet.

PRAYER

S. Luke xi, 13.

Our Lord speaks. ' Often you have asked me, my children, how to pray, and I have shewn you. Prayer is intercourse with God. It is the cry of our hearts to God. So that it must be something perfectly natural, perfectly genuine, the expression of the deepest things in your heart. It is not your lips that should speak, nor your mind, but your will. Your will manifested, spread out before your

MEDITATIONS OF A HERMIT

Father, true, naked, sincere, simple, and presented before him by you. This is what prayer should be. This needs neither a long space of time nor many words, nor many thoughts. It varies: sometimes it will be longer, sometimes quite short, according as your heart's desire prompts you. If it is quite simple, a word will express it. If it is less simple you will need longer phrases to explain it. In any case, it is the attitude of your will that you express, or the attitude of your heart, if you like, but not your heart with all its imperfections, its disordered affections. No, it must be your heart corrected by your will, your heart as you would like it to be—emptied of all that you should not allow it to harbour, of all that you would keep away from it. Prayer then is to ask for what you desire, but for what you desire by the help of grace and in the sight of God.

'Pray thus, desire only that which I desire, according to my desire and in the measure that I desire it. *Thy Will be done.* This will be your prayer for all Eternity in Heaven.

'All the Will of God and therefore all your own desire, all that God wishes and all that you can wish is held in those words: "Thy Will be done."

'Prayer is all intercourse of the soul with God. It is also the attitude of the soul when it contemplates God without words, solely occupied in contemplation, speaking its love with constant regard, though lips are silent and even thoughts are still. *The best prayer is the most loving prayer.* The more it is laden with love, the more the soul holds itself tenderly and lovingly before its God, the more acceptable is that prayer. Prayer, in the widest sense of the word, may be either a silent contemplation or one accompanied by words. Words of adoration, love, self-immolation, the giving of all one's being, words of thanksgiving for the graces and blessings of God, for favours shewn to oneself, or to others, words of regret in reparation for one's sins or those of others, words of supplication.

' My children, what I ask for you in your prayer is love, love, love. Besides the time that you should consecrate entirely to prayer every day, you should lift your hearts to me as often as possible. When at work, you can, whilst giving yourself up to it, either keep me constantly in your thoughts as is possible in purely manual labour, or perhaps you will only be able to lift your eyes to me from time to time, whenever you can. It would be sweet and right to contemplate me always, never to lose sight of me—but this is not possible in this world, for ordinary men ; it is only possible in Heaven. What you can and should do is to lift your hearts to me as often as you can during the time that is not taken up solely with prayer ; lift the eyes of your soul up to me as often and as lovingly as you can, and whilst you are at work keep the thought of me as much present to your mind as is compatible with your work. Thus you will be praying ceaselessly, continually, as far as it is possible for poor mortals to do so.

' *Praying*, you see, is above all to think of me with loving thoughts ; and the more you love, the better you pray. Prayer is to have the attention lovingly fixed on me. The more loving the attention the better the prayer.'

HOLINESS

' And you, my cherished ones, my chosen ones, my privileged ones, my Beloved ones, remember, you my elect, those warning words I spoke : " From him that hath received much, much will be required." It was for you that this was spoken. You, my chosen, you, my spoilt ones, you to whom I have told everything, given everything, you who have had so many graces. The more you have received, the more will be asked of you. The very greatness of the favours I have given you is a sign that I will give you myself in the measure of holiness that I ask of you.

'Never then be foolish enough to think that it is pride on your part to desire, hope and wish to attain to great holiness. It is, on the contrary, your duty. You cannot fail to recognize the graces I have poured out upon you and perceive that they themselves are a command from me to rise to great heights of holiness : when I give much grace to a soul it is as though I were to say to it : " I wish you to become very holy. I shall ask of you an account of these graces that I give you."

'My favour and grace poured out on you should only make humility and fear grow in you. Far from being proud, the more you receive the more will you be filled with fear and humility in the sense of your deep lowliness. What you have to fear more, if you are of a right mind, is not so much pride as discouragement, and this would surely come if I had not enjoined on you the duty of hoping always in my infinite mercy, and of throwing yourself in your desperation upon my heart, however poor and wretched you may feel yourself to be, as the Prodigal Son threw himself upon the heart of his father.'

EIGHT DAYS AT EPHRAIM

FOURTH SUNDAY IN LENT

6.30 p.m.

The day passes, my God. Alas, this stay at Ephraim is nearly over ! How quickly the time goes ! In three weeks at this hour you will be *Risen.* What a word ! How it overwhelms one ! How blessed and glorious for the Holy Trinity ! All your sufferings, all your labours will then be over. For all Eternity you will be the King of Glory. With what impatience and joy I should welcome this day, if it were not that you must go through such great sufferings before it comes. Alas, you enter into your glory through such sufferings ! The thought of them freezes my heart and a chill as of death invades me. O my Lord Jesus, your last day will be a Friday, the Friday a fortnight hence. Let it come then and let your children console you these last days that remain. O my God, let me console you all the days of my life, may all your children give you consolation, and may your will be done in all things. Amen.

THE NARROW WAY

' Enter by the narrow path, for the broad path leads to destruction.' That is to say, go in by the way of mortification, of obedience above all and penance, for the other way, the easy way of soft living, of ease and independence, leads to Hell. Amongst many other snares in life you have to avoid those that I have so often pointed out to you, saying : "Avoid the leaven of the Pharisees and Sadducees."

' *The Snare of the Pharisees* lies in seeking perfection

indeed, but trying to find it in purely exterior observances and minute formalities rather than seeking it in practical virtues and imitating my example. This obstacle throws one into hypocrisy, rash judgements, hardness of heart, an abyss in which the soul is engulfed.

' *The Snare of the Sadducees* is that laxity which, under the pretence of setting store only upon interior holiness, rejects all exterior practice and all which irks the body, declaring all mortifications to be useless. Thus one becomes the slave of one's senses, incapable of submitting either soul or body to obedience and rejecting all crosses and humiliations. Now I will trace for you the way between these two snares. Take *the narrow way!* This narrow way I have shewn you elsewhere. This narrow way is the way of my own example, the way that I pointed out when I said : " If anyone will follow me let him deny himself daily and imitate me." Do this, my children, and you will live and follow me in this path, taking care not to fall into the two traps of pleasure and seductions.'

8 *p.m.*

My Lord Jesus, the night has fallen ; all is quiet, the earth is wrapped in silence and shadow. The village is asleep, no sound is heard. You are watching. Your Mother, S. Mary Magdalen watch with you and contemplate you with sadness, praying for you. They count the days : eighteen days till your Passion, nineteen till your Death. You, dead, my Jesus, you, Life itself! And dead in such torments! And by your own will! And with the consent of your whole heart. Your Sacred Heart thirsts to be baptized with this Baptism. Our own heart faints at the thought of it. My God,

EIGHT DAYS AT EPHRAIM

I see approach me the end of the life you lived for thirty-three years on earth. How quickly it has gone by. With what ineffable sweetness you have filled it for me, what precious graces you have poured out on me and upon us all who surround you, and over the whole earth! Shall I say what once was said to you : ' Please God that you may not have to suffer so, my Lord.' No, I have no other will but thine, my Saviour. I have given you once for all my will ; I will never take it back ; it is for ever lost and sunk in your will. May all your will be done! May all be accomplished as you wish. Thy will be done, my God! I know that your will is your glory and your good. Thy will be done! O my God, let me and all those whom you have put under my care, may all the faithful of the Church, may all men in all things do your will!

THE GOOD SHEPHERD

Our Lord speaks. ' I am the Good Shepherd, I seek my lost sheep without ceasing. I have said to you again and again : " Love me." For as I have loved you all, my sheep, so should you love one another for the tender love that your Shepherd bears you. Be grateful to me for my care in seeking you, my goodness in forgiving you, my joy in finding you. Help me in this work, imitate me. Do all you can like me and with me (each one under obedience to his spiritual director) to bring back the lost sheep to the fold. Share my grief when my sheep go astray, and my joy when I find them again. Share my faithfulness, my hope, my indulgence, in seeking them, my hope which never gives up believing in the possibility of their return, my indulgence in pardoning them. Share my tenderness for them when they return. I do not reproach and punish them. Far from this, I caress and embrace them as the father did the Prodigal Son. *Hope then always* for the return of all souls living in this world ; work for it always so far as obedience allows you, and shew tenderness to the sinners who return as I did to so many souls. In this command is all contained, *Do for sinners as you would that I should do for you.*'

MONDAY AFTER THE FOURTH SUNDAY IN LENT

' My children, the day is almost over. I have only a few words to say to you. My time is almost fulfilled and this Retreat at Ephraim is nearly over. To-morrow morning we will go to Galilee, but I have still three things to say to you while we are here together in solitude.

'First, poverty, poverty, poverty. Remember my example and my words about poverty. I was born in a stable and brought up in a poor cottage. My parents were poor and I lived poorly by the labour of my hands until that day when I gave up my time to preaching. Since that day I lived by the alms of the faithful, but would take only that by which I could live as simply as when I was a labourer. I had no possessions in the world nor even a stone to lay my head upon. I chose my companions, the apostles, from amongst the poor, and preached poverty. Remember my words : " Blessed are the poor." " Woe to the rich." " If you would be perfect, sell what you have and give it to the poor." " If you do not renounce all, you cannot be my disciples." " You cannot serve two

NOTES ON THE SPIRITUAL LIFE

masters, and cannot love God and money both together." "The poor man Lazarus was carried by angels to Abraham's bosom." Those who leave all to follow me receive a hundredfold in this world, and in the next Life everlasting. I would not let this day end without repeating again : *Poverty, Poverty, Poverty*, Faith in Prayer . . . Humility.'

NOTES ON THE SPIRITUAL LIFE

1897–1900

These notes were found in two manuscript books with the above title written on them. They deal with many aspects of the spiritual life, and some of them are undoubtedly autobiographical. Others are thoughts suggested to Charles de Foucauld by his reading. We know that he read S. Teresa with particular pleasure, and also S. John of the Cross and S. John Chrysostom. He kept their works always by him, and after his death well-worn copies were found in his hermitage at Tamanrasset.

I

PENTECOST,

June 6, 1897.

My God, what is it that most displeases you in my soul ? I lack the spirit of prayer, of confidence in you, gentleness, fidelity, generosity. Our Lord cannot be pleased with me. . . . I feel only dryness and darkness . . . it is all painful to me : Holy Communion, prayer, meditation, all and everything, even just telling Our Lord that I love him. I must hang on to the life of Faith. If, at least, I could

MEDITATIONS OF A HERMIT

feel that Our Lord loves me. But he says nothing. What I lack above all is self-forgetfulness and a brotherly feeling towards others. . . .

'You ask what displeases me most in you. . . . This, that you do not love me simply enough . . . entirely enough, because you love yourself too much and others for your own sake and theirs. Do nothing for yourself or for others out of love of yourself or love of them. In all you do, see only me. In all you do, ask always " What would my Master do ? " and do it yourself. Thus you will love only me, thus I will live in you. You will lose yourself in me and live in me, you will have lost yourself, and my Kingdom will be begun in you.

Your vocation. It is to preach the Gospel in silence as I did in my hidden life, and like Mary and Joseph.

Your rule. To follow me, to do what I should do. To ask yourself always " What would Our Lord do ? " and to do it. This is your only rule, but it is absolutely your rule.

Your spirit. Love of God and forgetfulness of self in joyful contemplation of my glory ; compassion and grief for my sufferings ; joy in my joy ; grief for sins committed against me, and a burning desire to see me glorified by every soul. Love of your brother for my sake who love all men as a father loves his children. To wish for my sake for the spiritual and material good of all men. Freedom, liberty of speech, tranquillity, peace. All for God's sake, nothing for your own sake or any other creature's.

Your prayer. First method. (1) What have you to say to me, my God ? (2) This is what I have to say

NOTES ON THE SPIRITUAL LIFE

to you. (3) Keep silence with your eyes fixed on the Beloved.

Second method. *Quis, quid, ubi, quibus auxiliis, cur, quomodo, quando.*

At Mass. Divide it into three parts :

1. As far as the consecration, offer me to my Father and recommend your intentions to him. Thank me for my cross and ask pardon for making it necessary.

2. From the consecration to the communion, adore me upon the altar.

3. After communion, adore me within you, thank me, love me, rejoice, be silent.

Your thought of death. Think that you may die a martyr, despoiled of everything, stretched on the ground, covered with blood and wounds, violently and painfully killed. Wish this to happen to-day. If I am to give you this infinite grace, be faithful in watching and in carrying the Cross. Consider that such a death should be the object of your whole life ; see in it how little other things matter. Think often of this death so as to be ready for it and to judge things at their true value in the light of it.'[1]

I ask for no consolations from Our Lord (in the first place, I deserve none), for it would be such joy for me to hear him speak or to feel him in the depths of my heart that it would be like Heaven, and one cannot have Heaven both in this world and the next. I ask only one thing : to be faithful to him. I, who am so unfaithful. It is right that

---

[1] Charles de Foucauld wrote this in 1897. Nineteen years later, December 1st, 1916, he was assassinated by the **Senoussi** at Tamanrasset.

a soul with so little fervour should feel no sweetness. God sometimes allows such darkness that not a star seems shining in it. These are the times at which one must remember that we are in the world to suffer and to follow Our Lord in this dark and thorny path. We are pilgrims and strangers upon earth. Pilgrims must rest in tents and cross deserts, but the thought of the Promised Land makes them forget these things. Here we are in a strange land, we must hang up our harps and weep.

In everything I desire only the holy will of God. Alas, I love my Lord so ill that I dare not call him my Beloved ! Nevertheless, I long to love him more than all in heaven or earth. I give my heart and my life to him.

' When you are sad, tired, lonely and full of suffering, take refuge in the sanctuary of your soul and there you will find your Brother, your Friend, Jesus, who will console you, support you and strengthen you.'

' All is summed up in this, my son : lose yourself and you will find yourself.'

I am content now in my cherished solitude, far away from the world where he is so often offended. We are happy in solitude with him, alone with his love, alone with his lovingkindness. He knows that I love him.

Since the sin of Adam man can no longer do any material or spiritual good on earth without suffering in proportion to the good he does. Because spiritual goods are of an infinitely higher order (since the love of God is the greatest of all prizes) they cannot be bought except at the cost of pain and suffering, suffering which becomes the greater as we aim

NOTES ON THE SPIRITUAL LIFE

higher. The darkness and suffering of soul which we experience in the life of divine love, are crucifying in the measure in which they can, so to speak, be bartered for the price of divine love, that supreme prize. That is why we can only attain to loving God on the condition that we purchase love with darknesses and sufferings proportioned to the degree of love to which we shall attain.

We should long for all men to be in a state of grace, desire that all men's souls, as many as there exist in the world, should become living tabernacles of God's grace. We should long that all souls in a state of grace should sanctify themselves to the utmost and be inspired by Jesus to acts by which each gives infinite glory to God.

Election. (November 14, 1897. Feast of the Patronage of the Virgin.) I resolve by God's grace to attain to complete detachment from all that is not God, to poverty of spirit which permits of neither mean thoughts nor worries nor anxieties, either spiritual or material, nor small calculations, nothing worldly, small or vain; to empty my soul of all this and live only in the thought of God's love. To live on the heights, to live in heaven like Mary Magdalen at Sainte Baume.

2. I resolve to cure myself of the fear I have of the Cross and to be more generous in mortification. To love God with a perfect burning love.

NAZARETH,
April 26.

To follow Jesus crucified, I must lead the life of the Cross.

MEDITATIONS OF A HERMIT

I have perfect confidence that if I am faithful the will of God will be accomplished not only in spite of obstacles but because of them.

Obstacles are a sign that God is pleased with something. The weakness of human means is a cause of strength to him. God uses adverse winds to blow us into port.

Often the words of Our Lord to S. Teresa encourage me in my cowardice and human respect. 'Either I shall be glorified or you will be despised. In either case you will be the gainer.'

I have a deep and growing conviction that to glorify God and 'do here on earth the work of the Heavenly Father' I must taste of the Cross that Jesus left as his example.

LETTERS WRITTEN BETWEEN 1897 AND 1900

To a Trappist

NAZARETH,
September 30, 1897.

We should try to be so closely united to Our Lord that we reproduce his life in our own, that our thoughts and words and actions should proclaim his teaching, so that he reigns in us, lives in us. He so often enters within us in Holy Communion. May his Kingdom reign in us.

If he sends us happiness let us accept it gratefully. Like the Good Shepherd he sets us in a rich pasture to strengthen us to follow him later into barren lands. If he sends us crosses let us embrace them and say '*Bona Crux*,' for this is the greatest grace of all. It means walking through life hand in hand with Our Lord, helping him to carry his Cross like Simon of Cyrene. It is our Beloved asking us to prove how much we love him. Whether in mental suffering or bodily pain ' let us rejoice and tremble with joy.' Our Lord calls us and asks us to tell him of our love and repeat it over and over again all through our sufferings.

Every cross, great or small, even small annoyances, are the voice of the Beloved. He is asking for a declaration of love from us to last whilst the suffering lasts.

Oh, when one thinks of this one would like the suffering to last for ever. It will last as long as Our Lord wishes. However sweet the suffering may become to us, we only desire it at such times as Our Lord sends it. Your will be done, my Brother Jesus, and not mine. We long to forget ourselves, we ask nothing, only your glory.

' Hallowed be thy name, thy Kingdom come, thy will be done ' in all men, and in us, so that we may praise you with all our powers all through life, consoling your Sacred Heart, doing your will. This is all we can desire, all we need. See, we are at your feet, do with us as you will ; whatever it may be, we have no wish or desire but to do your will.

To a Friend

December 26, 1897.

Let us thank God a thousand times if in the sadness which invades us it seems to us as if we are rejected by the world. The depression and suffering, the bitterness with which we seem sometimes to be soaked, were the lot of Our Lord on earth. Are we not fortunate to share them ? We should pity the happy people. Pity those whose happiness, even though it be quite legitimate and innocent, keeps them attached to the world. God is good that he has so despoiled us of everything, that we can draw breath only by turning our heads towards him. How great is his mercy, how divine his goodness, for he has torn everything from us in order that we may be more completely his. So the sufferers are the happy ones through the goodness of God. In suffering I give thanks. May these days of Christmas festival bring you, in your suffering, I do not say consolation, but the blessing God intends for you. The Child Jesus will perhaps not give you any sweetness,—he reserves that for the weak ones,— but his hands will none the less be spread to bless you in these days of Christmastide, and whether you feel it or no, he will pour abundant grace into your soul.

To his Sister

January 31, 1897.

It is good, is it not, to give oneself up altogether to the Sacred Heart of Jesus and to let him do everything for us, and to remember that whatever happens, except, of course, sin, happens by his will, that even sin is ' permitted ' by him, and that one can and should get good out of everything, even one's faults. It is good to feel we are in such kind hands, and lean on his Sacred Heart. It seems as though Our Lord cannot shew us enough love and power and wisdom, whether he shews himself as Father, or Brother, or Spouse. We are indeed blessed, we poor little creatures. God is very good to us.

Misericordias Domini in aeternum cantabo : I should like to say nothing else all the rest of this life, as in the next they will be my only words. Let us melt away, let our thoughts dissolve into praise and thanksgiving over the goodness of God for all men, his incredible love for each one, tell ourselves as we contemplate it that we are one of those little creatures he so loved that he lived and died and shed his blood for each of us. What love his was, and how happy for us to be so loved, and by whom? By infinite Beauty himself. What are we to be so cherished by God? It is good to speak of these things together and so to live together for a few moments the life of Heaven, waiting till by God's mercy we share it for Eternity.

To a Trappist
Monday after the Ascension, 1898.

Your business now is to live alone with God and to be, until your ordination, as though you and God were alone in the universe. One must cross the desert and dwell in it to receive the grace of God. It is here one drives out everything that is not God. The soul needs to enter into this silence, this recollection, this forgetfulness of all created things by which God establishes his rule in it and forms within it the life of the spirit, the life of intimacy with God, the conversation of the soul with God in faith, hope and charity. Later the soul will bring forth fruit exactly in the measure in which the inner life is developed in it. If there is no inner life, however great may be the zeal, the high intention, the hard work, no fruit will come forth; it is like a spring that would give out sanctity to others but cannot, having none to give; one can only give that which one has. It is in solitude, in that lonely life alone with God, in profound recollection of soul, in forgetfulness of all created things, that God gives himself to the soul that thus gives itself whole and entire to him,

MEDITATIONS OF A HERMIT

To a Trappist, studying Theology at Rome

NAZARETH,
June 21, 1898.

I hope your life goes on being more and more buried, lost, drowned in Jesus, with Mary and Joseph. You are now passing through a time that can be compared to the early childhood of Jesus. He was learning to read at the knees of his holy priests ; he was not yet working for the salvation of men,—except by the inner impulses of his Sacred Heart, which was always praying for them to God, he was not working for any soul in particular. He was a little child. He did not help S. Joseph in his work. He could not yet.

He was learning to read at Mary's knee. He sat at her feet, smiled at her, caressed her and kept good and quiet with his eyes fixed on her. This life was enough for him, the Son of God, for many years. Let it be enough for you. It will be yours for some years : it is as though you were five years old and were learning to read, like a child, and humbly and obediently do all you are told, just as Jesus at five years old did all that his parents told him.

Later he will take you to the desert . . . from there to Gethsemani . . . then to Calvary. But for now live with Jesus, Mary and Joseph as if you were alone in the world with them in their little home at Nazareth.

To his Sister

JERUSALEM,
November 19, 1898.

When one is very sure that something is the will of God, it is so sweet to do the will of the Beloved that nothing else counts. He is here as he was at Nazareth. He is everywhere. What does it matter where I am? One thing only matters and that is to be where he wishes me to be, to do what pleases him most. Oh let us forget ourselves, forget ourselves, and live in Jesus, loving him with all our hearts ; for you know when one loves one lives less for oneself than for the Beloved, and the more one loves the more one directs one's life outward towards him one loves.

If we love Jesus we live much more in him than in ourselves. We forget our concerns so as to think only of what concerns him, and since he is in peace and ineffable blessedness, seated at the right hand of the Father, we participate, according to the measure of our love, in the peace and beatitude of our divine Beloved.

You ask me to pray for peace for you, my dear ; the secret of peace is to love, love, love.

Yes, I will pray for peace for you, or rather I will pray for the love of Jesus, who alone can be peace, and who gives it of necessity because he always brings it with him. Do you ask this too, ask for love, say ' I love you and let me love you more.' And think, say, do everything in the spirit of love. Do all that can rouse love in you, all that can lead others to love this divine spouse of our souls.

At times of sadness say your rosary, and meditate on the glorious mysteries and say to Jesus, ' Yes, here on earth I am poor and in misery, shaken by the storm and tossed by the tempest ; but you, Jesus my love, are risen again and you will never know suffering any more. Now you are happy for ever, you, Jesus my spouse. You are seated in the glory of the Heavens in perfect felicity. Is it myself that I love or is it you ? Oh, it is not indeed myself that I wish to love, it is you, my Beloved. You are in eternal bliss ; what do my troubles matter ? I want only to bless you, my Beloved. You are happy, so am I happy. How can I complain when my Beloved is happy infinitely and for all eternity ? '

To a Trappist

September 9, 1898.

I embrace and bless a thousand times your will, my Beloved, as it is manifested by my Superior. You deign to make me know your will through the voice of your representative, placed here for this purpose by your spouse the Church. Thank you from my heart, my Jesus ! What grace and favour you shew to this child of yours. How glad I am, my Beloved, to know your will, whatever it is, and to be able to do it. Thank you, thank you for all, whatever it may be. To do your will is my heaven here below, O my Jesus. Only give me the grace to do it perfectly, and forgive me that in the past I have made so little use of this joy.

To a Trappist
(*about the death of one of his superiors*)

NAZARETH,
December 29, 1898.

MY VERY DEAR FATHER,

I received this morning your letter of December 18, telling me this crushing news. Yes, we are left fatherless, both of us, for he was a father to us. Yet we have in the tabernacle him who said ' I will not leave you Fatherless.' And is our dear Father Louis dead himself? God forbid. He is more alive than we, more our father than ever,

LETTERS WRITTEN BETWEEN 1897 & 1900

he watches over us better than ever. I was expecting him every day. He wrote to me that he would surmount all difficulties to come to see me during his journey. Since the beginning of the month, whenever a carriage passed, or there was a knock at the door, I have asked myself ' Is it he ? ' and now this morning come these three letters with this grievous news. You know how I am praying at Nazareth. Sometimes I think of his goodness, his gentleness, his kindness, and I cannot master my emotion nor my tears. Sometimes I tell myself that after this long beautiful life, full of merit, so full of charity, and helped by so many prayers and masses, he is already in heaven. And then I rejoice. I pray to him, and speak to him, and no longer feel separated from him, but, on the contrary, reunited to him by his having passed to the life of the saints.

Dear Father, for you it is a hard blow. But I know you take it in the right way, with adoration and blessing. ' All is for the best for those who love God.' We shall find our dear father soon in the Heart of Jesus—(for all flesh is like the grass, which lives but a morning)—in our heavenly country. I shall think of you more than ever, my dear brother in Jesus. The sadder you are the nearer you will find me to you.

To his Sister

JERUSALEM,
December 17, 1898.

A Happy Christmas and a Happy New Year to you and to all your children. I shall pray my best to the infant Jesus for you all this great night of Christmas. Do you remember the Christmases of our childhood? I hope you have made a Crib and a Christmas tree for your children, for they are two of the memories that do one good all one's life. Everything that makes us love Jesus, that makes us love our home, is so healthy. These childish joys in which all that is most sweet and tender in religion is mingled with our family life are a happiness that last right on into old age.

But there will be far more lovely Christmases in Heaven. Make a Crib and a tree for your children and do all you possibly can to make their Christmas happy, that it may leave indelibly a sweet memory for them. But still more prepare them for Christmas in heaven, by sanctifying yourself all you can, and in bringing them up to be saints. Do not bring them up for the world. It is not worth it. It passes too quickly and is not worth our respect or esteem. We are made for something better than the world; our hearts thirst for more love than the world can give; our minds thirst for more truth than the world can shew; all our being thirsts for a life longer than it can hope for on this earth. Do not bring up your children for anything so despicable.

To a Friend

May 8, 1899.

I have returned to my life of 'the labourer, son of Mary,' abasing myself, humbling myself, praying rather than reading, settling down again into that dear 'lowest place,' that Cinderella life, working, serving, poor and hidden.

To his Sister

May 8, 1899.

Bona Crux! Through the Cross we are united to him, who was nailed on it, our heavenly spouse. Every instant of our lives must be accepted as a favour, with all that it brings of happiness and

LETTERS WRITTEN BETWEEN 1897 & 1900

suffering. But we must accept the Cross with more gratitude than anything else. Our crosses detach us from earth and therefore draw us closer to God.

To his Sister

NAZARETH,
July 21, 1899.

The events of this life have no importance, nor have material things. They are but dreams at a halting-place on the journey, and they pass like dreams and leave no trace. To see things as they really are we must see them in that great light of Faith which illumines our minds with a light so clear that we see things very differently from those poor worldly souls. The habit of seeing things in the light of Faith lifts us above the mists and the mire of the world. It takes us into another atmosphere, into full sunshine, into a calm serenity, into a luminous peace above the clouds and the wind and the storms, a region without twilight or darkness.

We must live by faith and believe that what, by grace, we hope for, we shall possess in glory. Let us love God who will be our infinite recompense, at all moments of our existence, in time and in Eternity.

To his Sister

NAZARETH,
September 1.

I am glad to know you are near to a church and the Blessed Sacrament. They are great graces, the Blessed Sacrament, the Mass and Holy Communion. It is a great grace to be at the feet of Our Lord, and to receive him. How blessed we are !

MEDITATIONS OF A HERMIT

And then God is with us always, within the depths of our souls always, always, always there, listening to us and asking us to speak to him sometimes. Give your children the habit of talking to the Divine Guest in their souls, remind them often that for us, Christians, there is no solitude : ' the desert has blossomed like the lily,' says one of the Psalms. That is quite true for us. God, our sweet Jesus is within us. We can take comfort in sitting at his feet, in contemplating him like Mary Magdalen at Bethany.

Oh, no ! Mary Magdalen was not alone at Sainte Baume. She was no more alone than she was at Bethany. But instead of having God visible before her in a mortal shape, she had him invisible in her soul, but he was no less present. She was seated at his feet here as there. This is my life too, dearest, as much as my weakness, my misery, my meanness, my lukewarmness, my cowardice will allow. Try to make it more and more yours. It will not deter you in your other occupations, nor separate you from others, it will take only a moment of your time ; only instead of being alone you will have a Companion in your work and your duties. Now and again lower your eyes to your breast and remain in recollection for a few seconds thinking ' You are there, my God, and I love you.' It will take you no longer than that, and all that you do will be the better for it, for you will have got help, and such help ! By degrees you will develop the habit, and you will end by always feeling this sweet companionship of the God of our hearts. Then there will be no more solitude for you. And we shall be more united than ever, for we shall be leading identically the same life.

We shall pass our time in the same manner with

LETTERS WRITTEN BETWEEN 1897 & 1900

the same dear Companion. We must pray each for the other that we may always keep company with the beloved Guest of our souls.

And let my example teach you that we can never say we shall be happier in one place than another, in some circumstances or others, for the very simple reason that it is God, the all-mighty Power of our souls, who gives us consolation and joy, where, when and how he will. In one moment he may destroy our dream of happiness ; in an instant he makes ' the desert to bloom like a lily,' and he turns the ' night into a glowing light,' as says one of the Psalms.

To his Sister

NAZARETH,
October 13, 1899.

Thank you for your good wishes for my birthday. Yes, I am glad to be forty-one, and glad to think my body is decaying and the end of the pilgrimage coming nearer. I am very well, but I hear the voice of the Prophet saying, ' All flesh is as grass and passes like the flowers of the field. In the morning it springs up, and in the evening it is dried up because the breath of the Lord has blown upon it.'

I thank God for giving you another child, another soul, a saint. What a happiness and what an honour ! Under whose protection in Heaven will you put this happy child ? Yes, dearest, I always do and always will pray for you more and more. Don't overtire yourself, don't worry. Yes, live very simply, avoiding all unnecessary spending, and detach yourself more and more in your way of living from all that is worldly and vanity and pride. These are stupid things. They only serve to diminish our future glory in Heaven, and to lengthen our time in Purgatory, and they make us responsible for bad example given to others. We should not take part in a way of living that even our natural reason condemns, and that is still more condemned by the Christian religion, and that we only adopt so as to do as others do. It would be far better to give a good example than to follow their madness. Yes, give up all that is useless, all that smells of the world. Don't fuss and worry for the future ! But give up nothing that can contribute to the moral and intellectual education of your children, and nothing that is useful to your own spiritual progress. Don't economize in books. If souls consecrated to God, monks who meditate on perfection from morning to night, feel the need, to the end of their lives, of reading and re-reading the works of the great Masters of the spiritual life and the lives of the saints, their forerunners, how much more have those the need that have to live in the world in the midst of so many distracting preoccupations.

Don't economize in almsgiving—cut off nothing in charities, rather increase them if anything. 'Give and it shall be given you.' 'In the measure that you do to others so shall it be done to you. What you give to the poor you give to me.' The best way of always having enough is to share generously with the poor, seeing in them the representatives of Jesus himself. And then be full of confidence. 'He who gives life will also give the nourishment. He who gave the body will give the clothing. Seek the Kingdom of God and his Justice (that is to say, perfection) and the rest shall be given unto you.' This is said for all Christians and not only for monks. Be full of confidence. Keep yourself from all anxiety. Bring up your

LETTERS WRITTEN BETWEEN 1897 & 1900

children well for God, and God will settle their future a hundred thousand times better than you can do it, or all mankind put together.

To a Trappist

NAZARETH,
January 28, 1900.

My dear Father, my dear brother in Jesus, here is Christmas come again. In the body I am at Nazareth, but in the spirit I have been at Bethlehem for the last month. As I write to you I feel as though I am with Mary and Joseph beside the Crib. It is good to be there. Outside are the cold and the snow, images of the world, but in the little cave, lit by the light of Jesus, it is sweet and warm and light. Father Abbot asks me what it is the Divine Child whispers to me all this month as I watch at his feet at night between his holy parents, when he comes into my arms and enters into my heart in Holy Communion. He says over and over again, ' The will of God, the will of God.' ' Behold I come. In the head of the book of life it is written that I should do thy will.'

' The will of God and the will of God through obedience,' this is what the beloved voice of the Divine Child gently murmurs to me.

To a Trappist

NAZARETH,
March 8, 1900.

It is good to empty one's memory of all visible things, and to fill it again with the hope of heavenly things. Even here how happy we are. There are many miseries, no doubt, our sins especially and

MEDITATIONS OF A HERMIT

the long procession of our imperfections and our weaknesses, but when one thinks that our beloved Jesus is always with us in the Tabernacle, that he is often on our lips, that he is always in our souls, what can we say when we see the Blessed Sacrament, but that this life has lost its darkness. '*Nox illuminatio mea in deliciis meis.*' This poor dark world is transformed and illuminated in the rays of the Divine Host, ' the Light of the World till the end of time.' Not for all, for, alas ! many remain in the shadow of death, but for us who are privileged, for us ' who are chosen and not choosers.' Ah, dear brother in Jesus, how lucky we are.

Tell me about your health. I shall not be troubled if it is bad. Life or death, health or sickness, are God's business and not ours ; whatever he gives us in this way is what is good for us. We need only always, always be glad.

To his Sister

NAZARETH,
February 12, 1900.

MY DEAREST MIMI,

I have just received the telegram sent off yesterday.[1]

You must have suffered greatly at the death of this child, and I grieve too at the thought of your grief. But I confess that I am full of wonder and am transported with joy and gratitude when I think that you, my little sister, you, a traveller and a pilgrim on earth, are already the mother of a Saint, and that the child to whom you gave life is in that Heaven for which we all sigh and to which we all aspire. In one moment he has been raised

---
[1] Charles de Foucauld had heard of the birth and of the death almost immediately after baptism of his sister's child Régis.

above his brothers and sisters, above his parents, above all mortal men. He has more wisdom than the wise. All that we know as riddles he sees clearly. All that we desire he enjoys. The goal to which we labour so painfully, to which we shall think ourselves only too happy to attain at the end of a long life of combat and suffering, he has reached at the very outset. Those marvels ' that the eye hath not seen nor the ear ever heard,' he sees and hears and enjoys. He swims for ever in joy and drinks of the cup of divine delights. He contemplates God in love and glory, amongst the Saints and the Angels, in the choir of virgins of whom he is one, and follows the Lamb, wheresoever he goes.

Your other children are travelling painfully towards the heavenly home, hoping to reach it, but having no certitude and with always the possibility of being shut out. They will reach it, no doubt, after many struggles and sorrows in this life and perhaps a long Purgatory. He, this dear little angel, the protector of your family, has flown Home with one stroke of his wings. Without grief, without incertitude, by the generosity of Our Lord Jesus, he enjoys for ever the sight of God, of Jesus, of the Blessed Virgin, of St. Joseph and of the infinite joy of the Elect. How he must love you ! Your other children can count on him as well as you as a tender protector. What a strength to have a saint in your family. What an honour and happiness to be the mother of an inmate of Heaven. I repeat I am full of marvel and astonishment when I think of it. One thinks the mother of S. Francis of Assisi happy because she was present at the canonization of her son ; a thousand times more blessed are you, for you have the same certitude as

MEDITATIONS OF A HERMIT

she, that your son is a Saint in Heaven, and you know it from the first day of that child's life, without having to see him pass through a life of suffering to attain to his glory. How grateful he is to you. You have given to your other children, with their lives, the hope of happiness in Heaven and at the same time a state subject to much suffering. To him you have given at once the true happiness of Heaven, without uncertainty, without delay, unmixed with any suffering. He is blessed indeed, and how good Jesus is to reward this innocent child with an immortal crown in ineffable glory without his having to fight for it. This is the price of Holy Baptism, of the Blood of Jesus. He has suffered and fought enough to have the right of saving his own without any merit on their part. His merits are enough to draw whom he will, when he will, into the Kingdom of his Father.

So, dearest, do not be sad, but rather repeat with the Blessed Virgin, 'The Lord has done great things for me,' ' they have called me blessed throughout all generations.' Yes, you are blessed because you are the mother of a Saint, because he, whom you bore in your womb, is already, at this very hour, glowing with the Eternal Glory ; because, like the mother of S. Francis, you have in your own lifetime the incomparable happiness of thinking that your son is a Saint, established for ever at the feet of Jesus, for ever resting on his Sacred Heart, in the love and light of the Angels and the Blessed.

To his Sister

February 14, 1901.

Let Régis always be remembered in your family conversations ; think of him, all of you, and never let his brothers and sisters forget him or pass him over in silence. Speak of him often as if he was alive. He is more alive than any of us here on earth ; he is the only one of your children truly and fully alive, for he only has true life, whilst we, alas ! may still lose it like so many. But our dear Régis will help us to attain it. I pray to him often with faith. I ask him to teach me to pray ; ask it of him too and teach your children to speak to him of their needs. He loves them so much and he is powerful with God !

No, dearest, I am not distressed about the religious persecutions, but I pray God to give me and others courage, the courage and virtue to bear them, and draw such profit from them as he wishes. For he only allows them. He, the All-powerful, who so loves us, for the good of our souls. ' Blessed are they who are persecuted for justice.' How can we be downcast when Jesus calls us blessed ? Does he not know better than we what is good for us ? Jesus, who loves us, allows this to happen, as he allowed his own death, persecution that pursued him from his cradle to the Cross ; as he allowed the martyrdom of his apostles and of an infinite number of Saints ; as he allowed the Just to be tried in many ways, not that they might die, but that Jesus might be glorified, and that souls should be purified by suffering. They thus have occasion to practise such great virtues that they enter the Kingdom of Heaven by the Royal Road of the Cross, which is the only one, since Jesus trod it, that leads to victory. Pray then, let us humbly ask for strength, virtue, love. Love above all, for it contains all and teaches all. And far from being downcast let us rejoice. Jesus says, ' When they calumniate you and persecute you, when they drive you out for

MEDITATIONS OF A HERMIT

my sake, then rejoice, for your reward will be great in Heaven.' Our reward is great even here on earth, for to co-operate with the sufferings and persecutions of Jesus is a deep joy which one feels according to one's love for Jesus. Love longs always to imitate.

PART III

THE PRIEST, THE HERMIT IN THE SAHARA

CHARLES DE FOUCAULD was ordained priest by Mgr. Bonnet, Bishop of Viviers, on June 9, 1901.

He decided to continue his hermit's life, though no longer in Asia, but amongst the most abandoned of pagan peoples. He left for Africa at the beginning of September 1901, and established himself at Beni-Abbès. He was then the only priest within an area of four hundred kilometres. He lived on bread and barley soup; he slept on the ground, and prayed night and day whilst devoting himself to all around him. In 1904 he went still further into the desert, and settled at Tamanrasset, amongst the Tuaregs of the Hoggar. There he died during the Great War on September 1, 1916, assassinated by a Mohammedan tribe who were afraid of his influence as a priest and a Frenchman.

In a letter to the Abbé Caron,[1] director of the *petit séminaire* at Versailles, dated April 8, 1905, the hermit of Beni-Abbès gave his reasons for his choice. We print it here, as a preface to the various spiritual writings which belong to the years 1901 to 1916.

April 8, 1905.

I am an old sinner, who, after his conversion, nearly twenty years ago, was given a powerful

[1] See Abbé Max Caron, *au Pays de Jésus Adolescent*. Paris, Hâton, 1905, chap. vii.

MEDITATIONS OF A HERMIT

attraction by Jesus to lead the life he led at Nazareth. Since then I try to imitate him, alas ! very badly. I lived several years in that dear, blessed Nazareth as servant and sacristan in the convent of Poor Clares. I only left that blessed place to receive Holy Orders five years ago. As a free priest in the diocese of Viviers, I was shewn in my last retreats, before entering the diaconate and the priesthood, that it was my vocation to lead this life of Nazareth, not in the Holy Land that I love so much, but amongst the most sick souls, the most forsaken flocks. That divine banquet of which I am the minister, I was to give, not to my brothers and relations and my rich neighbours, but to the lame and the blind, to forlorn souls that have no priest to minister to them. In my youth I had explored Algeria and Morocco. Morocco is as big as France, and has ten million inhabitants, but there is not one single priest amongst them.[1] In the Algerian Sahara, which is seven or eight times as big as France, and has a bigger population than was thought at one time, there are, perhaps, a dozen missionaries. No nation seemed to me more abandoned than this, and I asked and obtained permission from the Prefect Apostolic of the Sahara to settle in the Algerian Sahara, to lead there, in solitude and silence, in holy poverty with manual labour, alone, or with other priests, or lay-brothers, a life that was as closely conformed as possible to the hidden life of Jesus at Nazareth. For three and a half years I lived at Beni-Abbès in the Algerian Sahara on the Moroccan frontier, living, very feebly and tepidly, it is true, this blessed life of

[1] To-day the French Franciscans and some nuns of the same Order, have begun to establish missionary posts and charitable works there.

THE PRIEST, THE HERMIT

Nazareth. Up till now I am still alone. ' The grain of wheat which dieth not remains alone.' Pray to Our Lord that I may die to all but him and his divine will. A little valley is my cloister, from which I never emerge except when duty calls me to carry the Blessed Sacrament somewhere, for there is no other priest, the nearest being four hundred kilometres away. For this reason I was obliged to make long journeys in 1904, but now I am back in my cloister before the Tabernacle living a life under the eyes of the Beloved as much resembling that of the Holy House at Nazareth as my wretched heart allows.

RETREAT BEFORE HOLY ORDERS

Corpus Christi 1901.   Notre Dame des Neiges.

Quis? (Who?). He who must follow and imitate Jesus the Good Shepherd who came ' to bring fire upon earth ' and ' save that which was lost.'

Ubi? (Where?). Wherever it is most perfect, not where there are the best chances of getting novices, canonical approval, money, lands and support, but where it is perfect in itself according to the words of Jesus, most conformed to the words of the Gospel, most in conformity to the works of the Holy Spirit, there where Jesus would go, to the sheep that have strayed, to the sick brothers of Jesus, to the more deserted who have the fewest shepherds, to those who sit in darkness, in the deepest shadow of death, to those in the power of the devil, to the blind and the lost. First to the Mohammedans, and Pagans of Morocco, and of the neighbouring countries of North Africa.

Quibus auxiliis? (Who will help?). Jesus alone,

MEDITATIONS OF A HERMIT

for ' Seek first the Kingdom of God and his justice and the rest shall be added,' and ' if you dwell in me and my words dwell in you, all that you ask shall be accomplished.' Jesus did not supply any help to his apostles ; if I do as they did, I shall receive the same graces.

Cur? (Why?). Because this is the way in which I can best glorify Jesus, love him, obey him, imitate him. Because to this I am urged by the Gospel, by my own inclinations and my director's counsels. So that I may make Jesus and his Sacred Heart and the Blessed Virgin known to the brethren of Jesus that know him not, and give the food of the Blessed Sacrament to the brethren of Jesus that have never tasted it, that I may baptize the brethren of Jesus who are still enslaved to the devil, and teach the Gospel, the story of Jesus and the evangelical virtues, the sweetness of the home that is our Mother Church, to the brethren of Jesus who have never heard of either.

Quando? (When?). *Maria abiit in montana cum festinatione.*[1] If one is full of the thought of Jesus, one is full of charity. Therefore, as soon as I am reasonably fitted, the Holy Spirit prompting, my director will tell me to go.

Would it not be better to go first to the Holy Land? *No.* A single soul is worth more than the whole Holy Land. I must go where souls have the greatest need, not to the holiest place. Is not this attraction, perhaps, a temptation of pride and self-love? No, for its results in this life will be, not consolation or honour for myself, but many crosses and humiliations. ' Either I shall be glorified, or you will be despised : in either case you will be the gainer,' said Our Lord to S. Teresa.

[1] Mary went up with all haste to the mountains. (S. Luke.)

ANNUAL RETREAT OF 1902

What proof have I that this attraction is the Will of God ? Two sayings of Jesus : ' Follow me,' and ' When you prepare a feast invite neither your brethren, nor your friends, nor your neighbour, who is rich, but call in the poor, the lame and the maimed and the blind.' (S. Luke xiv, 12-13.)

RESOLUTIONS DURING THE ANNUAL RETREAT OF 1902
BENI-ABBÈS

1. *Preliminary.* We must make the imitation of Jesus the whole work of our lives so completely that the words Jesus, Saviour, express ourselves as much as they are the expression of his nature. To this end we must be all things to all men, with only one desire : that is, to give souls to Jesus.

' Whatever you do to one of these little ones you do it to me. Let your light so shine before men that they may glorify God your Father.'

We must desire passionately to save souls ; do everything and arrange our lives for this purpose. The good of other souls must come first with us and we must do all we can to use the seven great means Jesus has given to convert and save the heathen,— the Sacrifice of the Mass, the presence of the Blessed Sacrament in the Tabernacle, kindness, prayer, penance, good example, personal sanctification. As the shepherd is, so is his flock. The good that a soul does springs directly from his inward life. So the sanctification of the people of these regions is in my hands, they will be saved if I become a saint.

If a man would come after me let him deny himself and take up his cross and follow me. Enter through the narrow gate ; choose the cross and follow our crucified Spouse, sharing his cross and his thorns. Let us seek sacrifices and cherish them as the world seeks after pleasure. If we do not accept our cross we are not worthy of Jesus.

'Seek the Kingdom of God and his justice and all these things shall be added unto you.' Be not concerned with how to live, what you will have to eat, nor for your body what to wear. We should rejoice greatly whenever we lack something.

I must divide my time for prayer in two parts. The first, at least equal to the other, I will devote to contemplation and meditation, the second I will give to prayer for all men, for all without exception, and for those with whom I am particularly concerned. I must say my office with great care. It is my daily offering of fresh flowers and roses, symbolical of fresh love offered daily to the Beloved spouse.

I will make frequent spiritual communions, unlimited except by my love, calling upon the beloved Saviour of my soul a hundred thousand times.

'He that heareth you, heareth me. He who humbles himself like a little child will be the greatest in the Kingdom of Heaven.' When in doubt incline always to obedience. Make acts of obedience wherever possible, not only because by so doing you can make sure of doing the will of God, but also in order to imitate Jesus in his submission in Nazareth and to obey his command to be like children. Also so that we may love Jesus in Heaven eternally, having that place reserved for us that is promised to those who put themselves lower than all, under obedience to other men, and practise the humility that this exacts.

I am in the house at Nazareth, between Mary

ANNUAL RETREAT OF 1902

and Joseph, embraced like a little boy, by my elder brother Jesus, who is present night and day in the Blessed Sacrament. So I must act as I ought in such company and in such a place, as I see Jesus act, giving me an example. In the Fraternity[1] I must be always kind and gentle and humble as Jesus, Mary and Joseph were in the house at Nazareth. Gentleness, humility, abjection, charity, and at the service of others.

I must wash the linen of the poor (especially on Holy Thursday) and clean out their rooms myself as much as possible. Do myself, and no one else, all the menial tasks of the house, keeping the parts occupied by the natives clean. I must take upon myself to serve them, so as to resemble Jesus who dwelt amongst his apostles as one who served. I must be very gentle with the poor and with all men : this also is humility. I must cook for the poor when I can, bring them drink and meat, and not leave this task to others.

In the sick I should see not a man but Jesus and feel respect and love and compassion for him, and joy and gratitude at being able to care for him with zeal and tenderness. I must serve the sick as well as the poor, striving to render them the meanest services as Jesus did in washing the Apostle's feet.

I should bear the presence of evil-doers as Jesus bore that of Judas, so long as they do not corrupt others. Do not resist evil. I should accede even to unjust demands upon me out of obedience to God in order, by so condescending, to do good to souls and to do to others as God himself does. I should continue to do good to those who are

---

[1] This is what he called his hermitage at Beni-Abbès, where he welcomed the visits of the nomads and the people of the village. He liked to call himself the brother of all men.

MEDITATIONS OF A HERMIT

ungrateful, to imitate God who showers his benefits upon the good and the evil alike. ' If you do good only to the good, where is your merit?' 'Do good to the bad and the ungrateful, and for your enemies, as God himself is good.' Every living man, however evil, is the child of God, made in the image of God, a member of Christ; to all is due respect, love, tender maternal care and great zeal for their spiritual welfare.

I need not wish to be able to give large alms in charity, this would be contrary to Our Lord's example. But, like him, I should live by the work of my hands and give what I can, like him, to him who asks or is in need.

' I am come to call not the just but the sinners.' It should be the one desire of my heart to bring Jesus to all men. I must concern myself specially with the lost sheep, the sinners and the wicked, and not leave the ninety-nine who have strayed to tend the one that is safe in the fold. I must conquer the severity and disgust that by nature I feel in the presence of sinners and let compassion, interest and zeal for their souls take its place.

I must desire and welcome with joy any suffering from cold or heat, or anything else, wish to be able to sacrifice something to God, to be more united to Jesus, to be able to glorify him by thus paying my tribute of suffering, and long to learn more and more in this world and the next to love and to thank him. The more we lack everything the more we resemble Jesus crucified. The more we cling to the cross, the closer do we embrace Jesus who is nailed to it. Every cross is a gain, for every cross unites us to Jesus.

I should possess no more and nothing better than Jesus had at Nazareth, and I should rejoice rather

NOTES OF A RETREAT MADE IN 1904

to have less than more. At every moment I should live as though that day I should die a martyr's death.

Only one thing is necessary : that is to do at every moment what is most pleasing to Jesus. I must prepare myself, without ceasing, for martyrdom, and accept it without the smallest attempt to defend myself, like the Divine Lamb, in Jesus, by Jesus, like Jesus and for Jesus.

I should rejoice rather to lack than to have, at failure rather than success, and at penury rather than possessions, for in these I bear the cross and the poverty of Jesus, the greatest blessing the earth can give me.

I must practise *Abjection*, the service of others. I must fix a certain number of menial tasks to be accomplished every day and to do them like Jesus of Nazareth, who 'came to serve.' I must do without the orderly[1] and serve, not be served.

NOTES OF A RETREAT MADE IN 1904

(1) *Point of meditation.* 'He went down with them and came to Nazareth.' (2) *Examination of conscience.* Are my spoken and my written words like those of Jesus of Nazareth ? Are they too many or too few ? Are they what they ought to be ?

Resolutions. To diminish (in general) the length of the letters but not their number : to talk (in general) at less length with everyone and to weigh my words so as to say what there is to say shortly and precisely. To speak more than I do of God and of Jesus. Talk more than I do to the children and less to the grown-up people. When in difficulties pray. When in doubt keep silence.

[1] One of the soldiers of the Garrison of Beni-Abbès had kindly come to do some manual work at the Hermitage.

MEDITATIONS OF A HERMIT

Sacred Heart of Jesus, I lay these resolutions before you and I pray you that this retreat and every moment of my life may be for your greater glory.

Mother of Perpetual Succour, I put myself into your hands, so that in life or in death you may always do what you will with me, carrying me in your arms, in this world and the next, as you carried the Infant Jesus, O my beloved Mother.

THE DETACHMENT, THE RENUNCIATION OF JESUS

'To him that would take your cloak give your coat also.' If I love Jesus I shall be attached to him alone, to his words, his example, his will. If I wish to possess him, to obey him, to imitate him, to be one with him, lose myself in him by losing my own will in his, all these things cry aloud the need for detachment from everything that is not him. The desire to possess nothing but him cries out: detachment. His words cry out: detachment. His example cries out: detachment. His will cries: detachment. I must resolve to see, unceasingly, Jesus in myself, dwelling within me with his Father.

I must work with all my strength to sanctify myself. Mortification, mortification, penance, death. It is when one is suffering most that one is most sanctified oneself and most sanctifies others. 'If the grain of seed dieth not it bringeth not forth. When I shall be raised from the earth I will draw all men after me.'

It was not by his divine words, not by his miracles, not by his good works that Jesus saved the world; it was by his Cross.

NOTES OF A RETREAT MADE IN 1904

The most fruitful hour of his life was that of his greatest abasement and annihilation, that in which he was plunged in suffering and humiliation.

Obedience is the measure of love : my obedience must be perfect so that my love may be perfect.

In order that I may work with all my powers to glorify God ; that in these distant pagan countries where none know Jesus, where the great feasts throughout the year, like Christmas and Easter, pass without a mass, without a prayer, without the name of Jesus being on the lips of a single man or woman ; in order that in these countries there should be tabernacles and priests, that many masses should be said and that fervent prayers should go up to Heaven and the Christian life spread its graces ; that on many altars the Blessed Sacrament should be exposed night and day and be adored by fervent religious, both men and women—the means to these ends is that I should sanctify myself as much as possible.

The hour in our life in which we are best employed is the hour in which we best love Jesus.

A soul does good to others not in the measure of its knowledge or intelligence but in that of its holiness.

For me, all men should be enveloped, in God's sight, in the same love and the same indifference. I must no more trouble about health or life than a tree troubles about a falling leaf.

I must remember only Jesus, think only of Jesus, estimating as a gain any loss at the price of which I have more room in myself for thought and knowledge of Jesus, beside whom everything else is nothing.

I must reserve all my strength for Jesus.

MEDITATIONS OF A HERMIT

SOME LETTERS
1901-1916

To a Trappist

NOTRE DAME DES NEIGES,
July 17, 1901.

I have thought constantly of you all through this my silence. Silence, you know, is quite the contrary of forgetfulness and coldness. In silence one loves most ardently; words and talk often extinguish the inward fire. Let us keep silence, dear Father, like Mary Magdalen and S. John the Baptist, and let us beg Jesus to light within us that great fire of love that made their solitude and silence so blessed. They knew indeed how to love. My first act on landing from the Holy Land was to go up to Sainte Baume. May Mary Magdalen, the beloved and blessed, teach us to love, and to love ourselves in Jesus, our All, and to be lost to all that is not he.

If I trusted to myself I should think my ideas crazy, but I trust to God who said, ' If you would serve me follow me,' and again and again he said, ' Follow me,' and ' Love your neighbour as yourself, and do to others as you would they should do to you.' My idea of practising this brotherly charity is to consecrate my life to helping those *brothers of Jesus* who lack everything, since they lack Jesus.

If I were one of those unhappy Mussulmans who know neither Jesus nor his Sacred Heart, nor Mary, our Mother, nor the Holy Eucharist, nor any of the things that make our happiness in this life and our hope in the next, and knew my sad state, how grateful I should be if someone would come and save me from it. So what I should wish for myself that I ought to do for others. 'Do to others as you would they should do to you.' I must do this for the outcast and abandoned, must go to the lost sheep and offer them my banquet and my divine food, rather than to my brothers and my wealthy neighbours (rich in all the things those unfortunate people are ignorant of), to the blind and the beggars and the lame, who are a thousand times more to be pitied than those who suffer bodily ills. And I see no better way to help them than to bring them Jesus, as Mary brought him to the house of John at the Visitation. Jesus, the best of all good things, the Supreme Sanctifier, Jesus who will always be present with them in the Blessed Sacrament. Jesus offering himself every day at the altar for their conversion, and blessing them every day at Benediction, is the best of all things to bring them. Jesus, our All. And at the same time, though I am silent, I can make known to those ignorant brothers of mine the meaning of our holy religion, and of the Christian spirit, and the Sacred Heart of Jesus, not by preaching, but by example and charity to all.

Let us love Jesus and lose ourselves before the Blessed Sacrament. There is our All, the Infinite, God. We should never forget what a gulf there is between the Creator and the creature; he is All, and we are nothing. When Jesus gives us overwhelming sweetness in his Presence, in contemplation, and the thought of him, let us not soil ourselves by the filth of passing things so as to deserve the reproach of Jeremias; *vescebantur voluptuose et amplexati sunt stercora.* Let us feed delicately from the hand of Jesus in love and contemplation and not sink to the *stercora.* Oh! could we but lose

MEDITATIONS OF A HERMIT

ourselves, sink ourselves, till death, in the ocean of the love of our beloved Jesus. Amen.

To his Sister

Saturday, June 14, 1902.

When will the time come for us to stand before Jesus and enter Heaven where his Sacred Heart would have us to be? What a blessed moment that will be. *Sicut desiderat cervus ad fontes aquarum; ita desiderat anima mea ad te, Deus.* As long as it is his will we should remain in this exile, let it be done and be blessed, but what joy when the time comes for us to lie on the bosom of our beloved Spouse. How sweet it will be to find ourselves above in the region of light and love. We shall love one another far better there, burning as we shall be with the fire of eternal charity.

July 4, 1902.

We can be so sure that dear soul[1] is happy and living in the light of the eternal love, that we have no need to be sad, but rather to rejoice together because she we love is happy. She has reached the place we would be in; she has arrived in that blessed port towards which we voyage in fear lest we should not be allowed to enter through tempest, and storm, and fear and pain. She is in that land of certain beauty, above the clouds of earth, lost in infinite light and infinite love. It is sweet to think of this joy of hers, and sweet, too, to think that most of those we have known are immersed like her in that boundless sea of love and happiness, and sweet to think that you will be there some day and even I am called there in spite of all my unworthiness.

[1] Charles de Foucauld is alluding to the death of a relative.

SOME LETTERS, 1901-1916

To a Friend

January 5, 1903.

You have had to suffer great loss and great grief. I would weep and lament your sorrow if I did not know that it is for your eternal good, and will gain you Heaven and eternal happiness, and that it is for this reason that your beloved Spouse Jesus gives such suffering to you. Though I give you deep sympathy, I will not pity you, for I know it is the Hand and the Heart of Jesus that gives you this bitterness now that he may load you with blessings hereafter in Eternity. May the will of Jesus be done in you.

To a Poor Clare

In our prayers let us ask him to make us love him, and that mankind may love him; or perhaps the best thing of all is to say to him every morning, that what we ask for ourselves we ask always for all men without exception. Then when we have said this we can leave others aside. We have done our very best for them. After this we need think no more of our fellow-creatures, but speak to the Spouse only of himself and ourselves as though we were alone in the world together. We can be *en tête à tête* with him, speaking only of our love. Let us lose sight of all created things after having done our very best for them in our morning offering. The more we forget men, the more we can do for them; the more we ask the beloved Spouse, in close converse with him, and forgetting all else but him, to make us love him with all the power of our hearts, the greater good we can do for humanity which shares in all our petitions.

MEDITATIONS OF A HERMIT

To his Sister

Beni-Abbès,
April 15, 1903.

Alleluia ! Life is like that ; all joy, even good and holy joy, passes, except that which has its source in God alone, and in his own infinite joy ; and even this may sometimes be hidden by divine permission from the most faithful hearts. It is only in Heaven that joy will be unfailing, and rejoicing, unchanging and perpetual. Let us join as far as we can here in the unchanging life of heaven. The dedicated can and ought to do so. Faith teaches us here what we shall there see clearly with our own eyes, and in the measure of our faith and our love we should be able to enjoy the immense glory of Jesus which is the joy of the Saints. Let us often remember that our Beloved is happy, and thank him for it with all our hearts.

Though we may suffer, our beloved Jesus is happy, that is enough for us, for it is him and not ourselves that we love. Though we are wretched sinners our Beloved is infinitely perfect and holy and glorious ; that is enough, for it is him, not ourselves, that we love.

Though those that we love here on earth (and we are bound to love all human beings as brothers) may suffer or sin, still our Beloved is happy and glorious in the highest heaven ; this should suffice, for it is him that we love ' with all our hearts and with all our soul, with all our mind, and all our strength, and above all things.'

Let us give him thanks unceasingly for his great Glory, as the Church does at the *Gloria in Excelsis* in the Mass. Let us join, even in this life, in the

SOME LETTERS, 1901–1916

chorus of Saints and Angels in heaven, and cry with them, Holy, Holy, Holy, Alleluia.

To his Sister
April 1903.

Sorrows and joys, consolation and trial, all come to you from the Sacred Heart, all is given by him for your very great good and your sanctification, and to increase your conformity to his will and your union to him. ' All is good to those that love God.' Hide yourself in the Heart of Jesus ; he is our refuge, our shelter, the house of the swallow, the nest of the turtle-dove, the bark of Peter to carry us over the stormy waters. He is happy now. He has no more suffering to bear. When you are in sorrow think of his happiness and tell yourself that it is his happiness that you desire and not your own, him that you love, and not yourself, and beneath all your suffering and sadness, and your anxieties and worries you will be able to rejoice in his joy and feel his immense peace. Let the thought of the peace he enjoys in the ' blessed and ever tranquil Trinity ' fill you in this world with happiness and peace whilst you wait for the vision in the next which will give you peace and joy for ever.

To his Sister
October 6, 1903.

I do not feel I want to talk to you of my hermitage, nor of my garden, nor of events. All these things are passing. Our settlements crumble away before they are even finished. It is absurd to speak of ' settling down ' for men who have but a day to spend on earth. Everything draws us towards the things of eternity, and it is of them that it is so sweet to speak. They mean home and reunion ; everything else seems meaningless.

To his Sister

BENI-ABBÈS,
Monday in Holy Week, 1903.

The more the soul forgets herself and gives herself up to the embrace of the love of Jesus, the more she enters into that peace of which it is said, ' Blessed are the peacemakers.'

To the Rev. P. Guérin, Prefect Apostolic of the Sahara

Wednesday in Holy Week, 1903.

Jesus is converting many souls. May the day come soon when the tombs are opened, and praises sound through all the heathen lands through which you pass.

To the same

February 27, 1903.

I am a wretched creature ; nevertheless when I search in my heart I find no other desire than this : ' Thy Kingdom come, hallowed be thy Name.' You ask if I am prepared to go anywhere but to Beni-Abbès to spread the Gospel. Yes, I am ready to go to the end of the world and live there till the day of Judgement.

Do not think that I hope by my manner of living to hasten the day when I shall rejoice in the vision of the Beloved. I ask only one thing, that which is his pleasure. If I love to fast and watch, it is because he loved it also. I envy his nights of prayer on the mountain heights, and love to keep him company. Night is the time for intimacy, the time for loving intercourse, the time for loving watching upon the Heart of the Spouse. Alas! I am so cold I dare not say I love; but I long to love; I long for this hour of intercourse at night; this is why I so love to watch and keep vigil.

I assure you that though I am far from killing myself (I am too much of a coward!) I will increase my *pulmentum* in obedience to you. And rest assured that for Jesus I am ready for all without reserve.

For myself I would ask you one thing only; pray that I may love; pray that I may love Jesus, that I may love his cross, that I may love the cross not for itself, but as the only way and means of glorifying Jesus. Only by dying can the grain of wheat bear fruit. ' When I am risen I will draw all men to me.' S. John of the Cross says that it was at his death, at the hour of his supreme renunciation, that Jesus did his greatest work, and saved the world. Then beg Jesus to give me the real love of the cross, because without this I can do nothing for souls. I am a coward about carrying my cross. People attribute to me virtues I am very far from possessing, though I have received so many graces. Pray then for me that I may love Jesus and be ready at all times to do his will.

To the Rev. Father Guérin

March 9, 1903.

What does the Sacred Heart of Jesus ask? I am the slave of the Divine Heart, but it is a slavery I never wish to break. I only pray the Beloved to rivet my fetters closer for all eternity. Tell me what is the will of the Sacred Heart.

MEDITATIONS OF A HERMIT

To one of his Nieces

November 15, 1903.

If a little nigger-boy was loved and loaded with good things by a great King, ought he not to give back love for love to this great King? The King is Jesus; we are like the little nigger-boy.

To a Friend

July 3, 1904.

If I was only faithful to the small duties of every hour, what good I should do. But because every hour I fail in faithfulness my work is fruitless and I remain alone. If I did my duty, I should win from the heart of Jesus the conversion of this people amongst whom I am living, who, for the first time, have the Blessed Sacrament in their midst, and many holy workers for the Gospel would join me. I beseech you to obtain this for me and also my own conversion.

To a Friend

February 18, 1905.

Our sufferings in this world are intended to make us feel our exile, to sigh for our home. They teach us to carry the cross of Jesus and share his life and to imitate him. They earn forgiveness for our sins and those of others, Heaven for us and for others, and they tear our hearts away from all creatures so that we may give them to the Creator.

To the Rev. P. Guérin

November 30, 1905.

I have just made my yearly retreat, and have asked for light from Jesus. The upshot of it is this:

SOME LETTERS, 1901-1916

I must do the very best I can for these heathen people in complete forgetfulness of my own self. How can I best do this? By the presence of the Blessed Sacrament, by the Holy Sacrifice, by prayer and penance, good example, kindness, my own sanctification. By using these means myself and by doing my utmost to increase the number of others who will use them also.

Since Jesus allows the hand of men to put many obstacles in the way of his work at this moment, try to get prayers from your people; prayer and sacrifice can obtain anything; no obstacle can withstand them, and nothing can prevent faithful souls from praying and suffering for your lost flocks.

To a Friend

August 26, 1905.

I shall stay alone, very happy to be alone with Jesus, alone for Jesus. Don't be anxious; we are both of us in the hands of the Beloved. He is a much better guard than all the soldiers in the world. Would you not be glad if I was to suffer the same fate as our great-great-uncle Armand;[1] would you not be glad? Jesus said there was no greater mark of honour. Would you not be glad to see me give it to him? But I don't think, all the same, it will happen to me . . . *non sum dignus.*

Pray that I may be faithful to that Divine Jesus that made himself lowly so as to bear me company in this little dwelling, smaller even than the house at Nazareth.

[1] Armand de Foucauld de Pontbriand, Vicar-General of the Archbishopric of Arles, was shot out of hatred for the Faith by Revolutionaries at the Carmelites, September 2nd, 1792.

MEDITATIONS OF A HERMIT

To a Friend
December 16, 1905.

From day to day I try to do the will of Jesus, and feel great peace within.

Don't be anxious at my solitude. Though I have no friend and no spiritual help, I do not mind my solitude, but find it very sweet. I have the Blessed Sacrament, the best of friends to whom I can speak by night and day, I have the Blessed Virgin and S. Joseph and all the Saints. I am very happy and want for nothing.

God gives a special cross to each one. I blush that mine should be so small. It shews I am a poor sort of servant, cowardly and weak.

To a Friend
January 15, 1906.

It will be good to get to Heaven after this life, full though it be with sweetness and a divine peace, as well as much suffering and many miseries and ills. There is deep peace and sweetness to be found if we plunge ourselves in the Heart of Jesus, and immerse ourselves in his pure love, and how great is the suffering as soon as we leave hold of it.

To the Rev. P. Guérin
April 2, 1906.

We are in God's keeping ! I am the happiest of men. Solitude with Jesus is the sweetest intercourse. But I long to do good, and to spread and to foster the truth. Anyhow, *non mea voluntas sed tua fiat.*

To a Friend
April 5, 1906.

How good God is to console men's hearts when he sees them nearly crushed by their burdens !

SOME LETTERS, 1901-1916

He knows so well how to mingle suffering and happiness in our lives ; sorrow enough to unite us to his cross, as much as each is able to bear, and then enough consolation to give back strength and refreshment to our tired souls and make them able, after a respite, to bear the cross again. He is tender and kind, and he arranges our lives for us so much better than we could do it for ourselves. We are so mean and low, such wretched dust, but he knows what is really for our welfare, and he knows how to provide for us. How blessed are we to be in the care of such a Shepherd !

To a Friend
July 15, 1906.

Now that life is almost at an end for us, the light into which we shall enter at our death begins to shine and to shew us what are realities and what are not. I love this desert, the solitude ; it is so quiet and so wholesome ; eternal things seem very real and truth invades one's soul. I am very reluctant to leave my solitude and silence for travel. But God's will be done whatever it may be, not only done but preferred, adored, loved and blessed without reserve.

To a Friend
September 4, 1907.

We can only have short hours of consolation and respite on this earth. May Jesus give you these if it is his will. With all my heart I pray him to load you with graces, to sanctify you and sanctify your children. I do not ask him to console you. He loves you far more than a poor human soul can love you, and knows so much better than we what

MEDITATIONS OF A HERMIT

is best. It is not for a poor humble sheep like me to give advice to my Shepherd. May his will be done in you whom he loves. This is the best thing my heart finds to ask for you.

My interior life is very simple. I see my path very clear before me. My work is to correct my innumerable faults and to do to-morrow the same thing that I do to-day, but to do it better. It is peaceful, but mixed with a certain sadness arising from pride and self-love when I see myself at the evening of my life, so wretched and bearing so little fruit.

To a Friend

November 18, 1907.

Does my presence do any good here? If it does not, the presence of the Blessed Sacrament most certainly does. Jesus cannot be in any place without radiating. Besides, contact with the natives familiarizes and instructs them, and gradually their prejudices and antipathies disappear. It is very slow work with very little result. Pray that I may do more good, and that better labourers than I may come to cultivate this corner of the Father's field.

In the Sahara, which is eight or ten times as big as France, and which, though it is not thickly populated, is inhabited all over, there are only ten or fifteen priests, all at El-Golea and Wargla. There are difficulties of every sort on all sides. It is hard not to be saddened at the evil that reigns, and the small amount of good, the enemies of God so active, his friends so hesitating, and oneself so feeble in spite of all one's graces. Nevertheless, one must not be cast down, but look, above all that happens, to our Beloved.

SOME LETTERS, 1901-1916

To a Friend

March 8, 1908.

I have a great devotion to Christmas, and the Flight into Egypt. I love in my comings and goings to think of this journey of Jesus and his parents, and to unite myself to him and try to imitate them in their contemplation and adoration and joy. We, too, have the Beloved always with us.

To the Rev. Père Guérin

June 1, 1908.

There is a word of Holy Scripture that we ought always to remember, which is that Jerusalem was built up again *in angustia temporum*. (Daniel.)

Difficulties are not a passing condition that we must allow to blow over like a storm so that we can set to work when calm returns. They are the normal condition. We must expect all our lives to be in *angustia temporum* as regards the good we wish to do.

To a Friend

June 4, 1908.

The whole country should be covered with religious, men and women, and good Christians living in the world, so as to establish relations with all these poor Mussulmans, to draw them gently, teach them, civilize them, and at last, when they have made men of them, make them Christians. You cannot convert a Mussulman first and civilize him afterwards. The only possible method is the contrary way and a much slower one, to teach and civilize him first and convert him afterwards. But to that end a great effort is necessary; not without a prolonged effort shall we bring to Jesus the four million Mussulmans of Algeria. In this

MEDITATIONS OF A HERMIT

part of the Sahara alone where I am, between this and Beni-Abbès, there are a hundred thousand souls. It is our duty to work for the good of each of these souls, if possible more for the Tuaregs than for the others. Souls have all the same price, which is that of the Precious Blood of Jesus, but since we cannot give ourselves to all, it would seem best to concentrate upon those that give most hope for good results: first amongst these are the Tuaregs, they are a young, strong, intelligent people.

To a Friend
April 9, 1909.

It would be too much sweetness to feel always that we truly love Jesus, that he loves us and that we are happy in his joy. If we always could feel this, earth would be Heaven. Let us be content with desiring and knowing that it is so, in this we have greater merit if less sweetness.

To the Abbé Caron
June 30, 1909.

Do not be surprised by the present storms. The ship of Peter has weathered many such. Think of the evening of that day when Peter and Paul were martyred. How dark everything must have seemed for the little Christian group at Rome. The early Christians would not let themselves be discouraged. And to us who have the life of the Church for eighteen centuries back to encourage us, efforts of Hell which Jesus said 'should not prevail' should seem very small and negligible. Neither the Jews nor the Freemasons can prevent the disciples of Jesus from working as the apostles did; let them imitate their virtues and they will have their success. Jesus says to us as he said to them, 'Go and preach the Gospel to all men.' We also can 'do all things through him that strengthens us.' 'He has conquered the world.' Like him we shall always bear the Cross, like him we shall always be persecuted, like him we shall always seem to be vanquished, but like him we shall always triumph in the end, and that in the measure of our faithfulness to grace, and in so far as we let him live in us and work in us and through us. We are with the All-powerful, and our enemies have no power beyond that which he allows in order to try us and sanctify us, and make us win spiritual victories, which are the only real ones, for the elect and for his Church.

We must come back to the Gospel; if we do not live by the Gospel Jesus does not live in us. We must come back to poverty and to Christian simplicity. After nineteen years spent out of France, what struck me most, in the few days I spent there, was that in all classes of society, even in very Catholic families, the habit and taste for costly and useless things had greatly increased, and I noticed an amount of worldly frivolity that was much out of place at such a grave time of religious persecution, and seemed out of keeping with the Christian life. The danger lies in us, and not in our enemies. Our enemies can only make us win great victories. But sin has its source in ourselves. The only remedy is to return to the Gospel.

To a Friend

July 31, 1909.

How I should like to see the faithful Catholics of France concern themselves a little with this

MEDITATIONS OF A HERMIT

Algerian people towards whom they have the duties of parents towards their children. For it is French soil, and it is dying under Islam.

To P. Guérin
October 31, 1909.

May Jesus grant great graces to the Sahara in 1910. For nineteen hundred years this country and these souls have waited for the Gospel.

To the same
February 4, 1910.

I shall do my best and God will do his will. Pray for me that my life may be such that he is able to use me for good. Happen what may, if my life is good, my time on earth will be useful to souls ; if I am bad or lukewarm, however I may labour I shall do no good.

To M. l'Abbé Caron
July 16, 1910.

Ah, yes, only Jesus is worth loving with passion. If calamity can shew us the truth of this, then the sooner the better, and the more completely, it is to be blessed.

To the Rev. Père Guérin
November 1, 1910.

Yes, Jesus is enough for us. Where he is nothing is lacking. Though those may be dear in whom we catch a reflection of him, still he is All. He is All in time and in eternity. How blessed are we to have this All that none can take from us, and which always will be ours unless we ourselves leave him.

SOME LETTERS, 1901-1916

To M. l'Abbé Caron
December 10, 1910.

We have Jesus with us, and however feeble we may be in his unconquerable strength we are strong. God has never failed mankind. It is man that fails God. He only wishes to pour out his Graces.

To a Friend
September 21, 1912.

Pray too for all the Mussulmans in our vast Empire of North-West Africa. This is an anxious moment for their souls, as it is for France. All these eighty years that Algeria has belonged to us, we have taken so little thought for the souls of the Mussulmans, that one might really say they have not been thought of at all. If the Christians of France do not understand that it is their duty to convert their colonies, it is a sin for which they will have to render account, and which will cause the loss of thousands of souls that might have been saved. If France does not administer her colonies better than she has done, she will lose them, and these people will relapse into barbarism, and lose all chance of conversion for ages.

To a Friend
December 4, 1912.

This holy time of Advent, which is always sweet to me, is particularly so here. Tamanrasset, with its forty little homes of poor labourers, is just what Nazareth and Bethlehem might have been in Our Lord's day.

MEDITATIONS OF A HERMIT

Letter written by Charles de Foucauld a few hours before his death, on the morning of December 1, 1916, to a friend.

Your sufferings, your past and new anxieties which you have accepted and offered to God in union with the sufferings of Jesus, are not only the sole things, but the most precious that God gives you in order that you may come before him with your hands full. Our own effacement is the most powerful means we have of uniting ourselves to Jesus and doing good to souls. This is what S. John of the Cross repeats at every line. When one can suffer and love at the same time one can do much, it is the utmost one can do in this world; one feels that one suffers, one does not always feel that one loves, and that is an added suffering, but one knows that one wishes to love, and to wish to love is loving. One knows one does not love enough, and it is true that one does not ever love enough, but God who knows from what clay he has made us, and who loves us more than any mother can love her child, has said, ' He who dieth not will not reject him that cometh to him.'

STRAY NOTES FOR MEDITATION

Watch and Pray. ' I invite you to spend the night in converse with me. Will you refuse ? '

' I ask you to stay awake to contemplate Me, to tell me that you love Me—to adore Me : to pray for all men : to ask pardon of Me for those who are sinning at this moment, and who stay awake for the purpose of sinning.'

If I neglect to stay awake and am too lazy to rise, (1) I am refusing to lay myself at the feet of Our Lord, and keep him company, we two together,

SOME LETTERS, 1901-1916

when he is calling me to do so. (2) I am preferring to sleep rather than to be alone with Our Lord, in intimate converse and union with him, the Spouse of my soul. (3) I am making a bad preparation for martyrdom. 'They answered him nothing.' They did not know what to say to their friend Jesus.

'They who in proud courage aspired to martyrdom
Are dumb : and soon will fly in confusion.'

Mortification. Through my cowardice over mortifying myself I am refusing to carry the cross. I am refusing to be a victim with Our Lord. I am refusing to follow him since he has said 'Veni.' I am refusing to help him carry the cross with Simon of Cyrene. Whilst he falls beneath the weight of the cross for me, and because of me, I refuse to touch it with the tip of my finger. I see him suffer and I let him suffer alone, I do not wish to suffer with him. I leave that to others and abandon him myself. I am resisting his invitation to my inner self, asking me to shew him some sign of my love. I am refusing to obey his orders, I who have so often told him that to obey him was my greatest joy. I do not love him enough to put myself out for him. I know that all suffering, all trouble that I take upon myself is a sign of love given to him : but I prefer to enjoy my ease to giving it up to him. For me, and because of me, he suffered cold, hunger, thirst, fatigue, labours, his Agony and the Passion ; and I seek to leave him alone to suffer and to spare myself all discomfort, all suffering of body or soul. He holds out his hand to me to walk with me, hand in hand, through life ; I let go his hand and let him go his way alone, and I on my side seek a less arduous way. He asks me to make him an oblation, a sacrifice, and I refuse. . . .

Lose my Life in God. The most perfect way. I should carry on in myself the life of Jesus: think his thoughts, repeat his words, his actions. May it be he that lives in me. I must be the image of Our Lord in his hidden life: I must proclaim, by my life, the Gospel from the roof-tops. *Veni.* My courage must be equal to my will. 'Seek thyself in me. Seek me in thyself.' 'It is time to love God.' Seek God only. Kindness. Gentleness. Sweetness. Courage. Humility.